FLIP!

ALMA LEIGH MOHR

Edited by Pamela D. Summers

Print ISBN: 978-1-54399-283-0

eBook ISBN: 978-1-54399-284-7

SYNOPSIS

Flip!; From fear to love. Flipping the channel on dysfunctional thinking, cultivating confidence and living a life fueled with joy and purpose.

Flip! was written for people who have experienced trauma, abuse, neglect, or any kind of adverse life altering experience at some point in their lives. These experiences often result as a life of neutrality, avoidance of conflict, people pleasing, tolerating toxic behaviors and poor boundary setting. These individuals typically have low self-esteem and lack of worthiness who feel trapped in their relationships, jobs, and personal goals. Flip! explains the difference between the fear-based mindset and the love-based mindset. Each chapter touches upon a dynamic that the reader is invited to explore in their own life by using the definitions and vignettes that are provided. While Flip! is organized by chapter, it is not linear. Like reading a dictionary, the reader can find a topic and read up on their lunchbreak without feeling overwhelmed with the construct of consuming a "front to back" self-help experience.

Flip! is beneficial to the reader because it is a stepping-stone in making significant life changes. Many people who are in a "rut" in life may feel depressed and/or anxious daily. While there are many legitimate mental health conditions that require the interventions of a professional therapist, there are also changes that a person can make in their life that will mitigate some of the causes of these conditions. Flip! addresses these issues and provides the reader with a sense of validation in their quest to live a better, more fulfilling life.

I am a licensed clinical social worker in the state of Colorado. I am the Regional Director of Psychological Health for the United States Air Force Reserve Command. I currently serve over 4,000 service members across the front range region of Colorado. I specialize in trauma therapy and have a specialty in military trauma and childhood sexual trauma. I regularly provide needs assessments to my members and referrals to therapists in the area where they serve. Many of my airmen present with issues that can be resolved with affirmative life changes. It's just that many of them feel trapped and isolated in their desire to effect changes in their own lives. Flip! is a journey that incorporates my professional experience but also my own personal experiences in overcoming a traumatic childhood. I am a veteran of the US Air Force Security Forces and am also a former Army wife. I am a mother to two awesome kids. I gladly demonstrate my vulnerability in my narratives as a measure to connect with my audience and incorporate my personal stories throughout the chapters. I have personally experienced these battles and I've worked diligently over the years to learn ways to overcome, survive and thrive past them.

This book is dedicated to my son Nick and my daughter Avery.

I learned how to love me because of you.

Thank you.

I love you Schlowski and Monk.

Mom

FLIP!

From Fear to Love: Flipping the channel on dysfunctional thinking, developing confidence, making amends and living a life fueled with joy and purpose.

Written by: Alma Leigh Mohr LCSW

Edited by: Pamela D. Summers

INTRODUCTION

Flip!

From fear to love: Flipping the Channel on dysfunctional thinking

Did you know that you have the power to live a life of purpose and joy without the need for external validation?

Did you know that you can eradicate the emotional pain caused by trauma from your life with no residual shame, guilt, or regret?

You and only you hold the key to your value and worthiness in your life. No one else can change, erode, or take away your worth.

It's ok if you're unsure. Read on:

Do you compare your life, job, marriage, appearance, intellect or other aspects of your life to other people and as a result feel inadequate?

Do you think that you deserve to feel less than others?

Are you hurting?

Do you tolerate toxic behaviors from people in your life?

Do you have a problem saying "no" to others without feeling guilty?

Has your own trauma / emotional baggage caused you to act in ways that has caused harm to other people and now you don't think you deserve happiness?

Are you caught up in a cycle of vengeful resentment towards those who have harmed you and those you assume to have intentions to harm you?

Are you fearful of change?

Do you want to live a life of joy and purpose?

Do you want to be more than just "ok"?

If you answered "yes" to any of these questions, you're in the right place, right now.

Before we go further know this: You are worthy. You are a beautiful soul with many gifts to share with the world. Your potential for joy in this life is immense and will be found when you simply believe. The first step is to choose to believe. You have the ability to choose. You have the ability to make positive changes. You can choose to release the pain in your heart no matter how deep. You will find purpose, strength and confidence as you move through these chapters. It is inevitable that as you read this book, you will identify with many, if not all, the topics. If you are hurt and traumatized by other people in this world, you will grow and learn how to move out of that negative space of anger. It takes time and you will learn how to give yourself permission to evolve and let go. Seems impossible? It's not.

How to use this book to your advantage.

I don't know about you, but I know that I can be easily overwhelmed or even disinterested in poring over a self-help book that drones on and on. This is not that book. I have segmented these chapters into digestible topics that you can pick and choose and read depending upon your mood and need. It is kind of like looking up a topic in a dictionary or encyclopedia. You want some perspective on Clarity? Head on over to that chapter. Need a pick me up regarding Worthiness? There's a chapter you can read on your lunch break. You can read it front to back as well. There are no rules in how you read this book. My intention is that you make it yours and use it for what you need when you need it. Flip through the chapters and find the message you need.

I have spent many years attempting to create this narrative and get it out of my head and onto paper. One reason behind my hesitation in doing so is I didn't feel equipped to share my narrative because I always felt so damaged and unqualified myself. It's funny to me now, knowing that my experiences have given me the very understanding that is necessary to embark upon this journey. We all deal with insecurities and those voices in our heads telling us that we are not enough. I am breaking through those notions and am putting pen to paper to share with you my revelations both from my professional clinical experience as well as my own personal journey. This life is not meant to be suffered. It is meant to be experienced with life affirming joy. Being ok is not ok. Ok is not enough. Every person holds a responsibility to themselves to be a good person and to do good things. We cannot be good for others and do good for others if we do not ensure that we are doing good for ourselves. We must enforce healthy boundaries and refuse to accept anything less than what we deserve. We are responsible both to ourselves and to everyone that we encounter in this life. Pain is unfortunate, but necessary in this journey. As Buddha says 'Pain is inevitable. Suffering is not."

Did you know that you can use your trauma to your advantage? When we recategorize our trauma as necessary, we can use the experience as fuel for our spiritual growth. Trauma is fertilizer, like manure. We can use it to capitalize and reach our highest potential. A soul cannot help another injured soul until they too have bled a little. Empathy is a learned emotion. If we do not suffer, we do not appreciate and understand the suffering in others. Your trauma can be a powerful tool to be repurposed for your greater good and the greater good of others.

I welcome this journey with you. With open arms and grateful acceptance, I openly share with you that I accept the fact that there will always be a part of me that will have scars. However, as I have developed a strength that has come from all these experiences, I want you to know that I'm going to share this with you because I believe that you are deserving and worthy just as much as I am.

While this is not necessarily an autobiography, there are many stories I will share in the following chapters to further illustrate my points and to express my deeply held feelings about what we do to ourselves and how we allow ourselves to be treated that is detrimental to our overall wellness and our pursuit of joy. It goes without saying that I am a student of life and, as to be expected, I have made many mistakes that I have learned from. My intention is to share what I have learned and give you the necessary validation and "sideline cheerleading" to help you grow, learn, heal, and thrive. Through my work as a psychotherapist I have noticed a pattern of issues that tend to arise when I am in session with my clients. These recurring themes are the foundation of this writing. Noticing patterns in human behaviors is also a recurring theme for me that has driven me to this composition. When there are patterns there is commonality. Ironically, a common pattern I have observed with my clients is the feeling of isolation, loneliness, and lack of self-worth and value. These are fear-based emotions and thought processes that could not be further from the truth, and in this book, I am going to show you why.

I deserve to be inspired and I also am responsible for being an inspiration to others. My hope for you is that once you read this book, either in its entirety or in bits and pieces, that it helps you move through a particular struggle or gives you the motivation to initiate real change as a means to better your life.

I didn't decide to become a social worker until my late 30s. It's an interesting take because the main reason that I became passionate about people and helping others was due in part to my experiences working for the TSA for several years shortly after 9/11. I was hired as a checkpoint supervisor, so that meant most of my day was spent observing and staying out of the way of my screening staff so that they could do their job without my interference unless they requested it. Occasionally, I would need to intervene with a rowdy passenger or decide on whether an item could be considered a threat to passengers in flight. It was an interesting job to say the least. I met so many interesting people, both in the staff that I worked with, as well as the countless people that I crossed paths with during my tenure.

Unless you have the time and resources available to travel the world, the next best possible place to meet people from every walk of life is in an international airport. There is an endless stream of diversity for you to observe. I noticed, albeit unintentionally, the subtle similarities of people. Often, I would observe the predictable nuances of human behavior regardless of age, gender, ethnicity or country of origin. Oftentimes, we assume that we are all so different. Perhaps that is true if you consider physical attributes such as race, gender, body type, and so on, but when you have the unique opportunity to observe behavior on a grand scale (such as a check point supervisor who is observing travelers day in and day out) you will begin to notice that, as human beings, we are all more similar than different. A simple demonstration of this would be to point out that we are all in need of toiletries and clothing and the necessary luggage used to contain all these necessities to make traveling easier. This is a simple observation. Granted many of those items are different sizes, colors, and quality, but as human beings we all have an inherent need for the same things. That observation grew into me noticing that at certain times of the day those individuals who did not take the time to show up early enough to get to the checkpoint would almost always behave in a way that projected their irritation onto the screening staff. Why was this? It was as predictable as the sunrise and sunset. From this experience, I grew increasingly interested in learning more about the effect of environmental influences on human behavior. The similarities in behavior led me to believe that we are so much more alike than we realize. I began to theorize that if we are that much alike, then whatever distress we experience must be far more common than we assume and therefore are more likely to be self-destructive and isolating simply because we feel so alone in our experiences. In other words, when I first began my job with the TSA, I was under the assumption that we are all very different and unique. However, during my time there my attitude shifted as I observed all these commonalities. So, if we are legitimately more alike than different, then would it not be a logical assertion that we are not as isolated and alone as we think we are? Bear in mind, these were just assumptions that I made as a lay person working a security job. I had not yet embarked upon my journey into clinical social work.

I was in my early thirties at this point in my life and had a young son to raise. I was working full time and finishing my bachelor's degree in criminal justice. I assumed that I would take that degree and pursue a different element of transportation security at some point in my life, not because it was a passion, but because it was my trajectory. I had spent five and a half years in the Air Force as a security police officer several years prior to me working at TSA and so it did not make sense to me to change career paths, at least not from a personal financial perspective. I felt incredibly grateful for the opportunity to become a supervisor with the TSA even though I had yet to complete my undergrad degree. Naturally, my expectations for the future were to continue pursuing new endeavors in a career that was centered around security and law enforcement. I had no idea that it would take me on such a remarkable journey of exploring and understanding human behaviors and helping and motivating others to live their best possible lives.

Many years later I was able to complete my masters level education as a clinical social worker and I have, quite honestly, loved it ever since. It is with this evolution that I want to share with you my observations and my own understanding of the basic reasons why people behave the way they do. I hope this book provides you with the insight and answers that you didn't know you were looking for. I hope in reading this book you can identify how your own patterns of behaviors have developed through your experiences, both positive and negative.

As I share pieces of both my intimate journey to wellness along with my professional insights, it is my hope that you find it encouraging, inspiring, funny, insightful, and validating. I hope that you take away the messages and lessons from this book that serve you. I encourage you to take time to conduct your own personal inventory and identify your beliefs and values. Consider what I have to say and take the time to decide whether or not you agree.

Do your own bit of investigation on who you are and what you think and feel. That's the purpose and intent of this book, after all. In these pages I will share with you my authentic belief about my own values as well as my own experiences. I hope that you will take them at face value and apply them to your own experiences with a little bit more understanding and a little bit more willingness to seek your own truth and your own joy in this life. I hope that you find clarity and I hope that you find a stillness in your heart regardless if your own pain is still there. I wish you resolution and recovery. I am grateful for you, the reader, for taking the time out of your life to digest these stories and lessons. I hope you enjoy them half as much as I have enjoyed sharing them with you.

CHAPTER ONE

FEAR AND LOVE

There are two basic emotions in the human experience; fear and love. All our emotional responses are secondary to either a fear response or a love response. You read that right. Every emotional response you have to a stimulus or trigger is rooted either in fear or in love. When we look back on our earliest experiences in life, we can decide on whether we were groomed to feel fear or to feel love at any given point in time. It is an element of survival to feel fear and as a result for us to react accordingly. When we are very young and are given all the necessary support and encouragement, then we feel love and we react to that as well. If a child feels loved, then they feel safe. When a child feels safe, they do not process fear as a primary response.

Picture this: It is as though we are sitting in front of a television that only has two channels. One channel is fear and the other is love. What we don't realize is that we have a choice and that we can flip the channel. This book will guide you on how to be aware of your choices in this life and how to cultivate joy based on an understanding of who you are and what you want versus what you have been groomed to believe about yourself. Sometimes we can change the channel and not even know that we are doing so. Sometimes we vegetate on the same channel without any awareness of what we are consuming nor any understanding that we have a choice and an ability to change the channel to something else, something better.

Have you ever caught yourself sitting in front of the television or computer watching a program that doesn't necessarily interest you or provide any positive influence? Do you ever catch yourself gravitating towards gratuitous entertainment to numb away life stressors? Much like consuming "junk-food" we can also consume "junk-entertainment" as well. Bear in mind that I am not judging. In fact, there is a time and place for all things. However, moderation is key. Do you ever find that you consume televised or social media content out of habit as opposed to exploring other more healthy, productive, and spiritually, enlightening options? The point is, what we often find ourselves mindlessly consuming, we also often engage in similar behaviors with regards to our sense of self and how we interact with other people.

Think of how you're manifesting your life choices through this lens. What channel are you watching? Are you in a relationship with someone that is watching the same channel with you?

Are you fearful of changing the channel and causing conflict with this person/people? Are you enjoying the shows on that channel? If you're caught up in a cycle of living in fear that is masked as anger, depression, anxiety, etc. do you have a desire to feel differently? Do you have a desire to make a better and healthier choices?

This book will not only encourage you to change the channel from fear to love but will also provide you with the ability to make that choice that maybe you don't know you have.

It has been said that most people fear speaking in public more than they fear death. This analogy is useful in helping us to conduct a personal inventory around our own sense of vulnerabilities. We must understand ourselves a little bit better before any personal recovery can be achieved.

So, as we begin, I'd like for you to take a moment to close your eyes and take a few deep breaths. Breathing deeply through the nose, being mindful of the expanse of your ribcage, hold for a few seconds longer, then slowly exhale through your mouth will cause your diaphragm to press down upon the vagus nerve which will engage a para-sympathetic "calming" response. When you've done this, we are going to explore and take inventory of some personal vulnerabilities. (Sounds like fun, right? It's ok. You're safe.) So, go ahead and close your eyes and take a few deep breaths. When you're finished come back to this reading to continue. Take as long as you need. I'll wait.

Now that you've taken a few moments to take some slow deep breaths I'd like for you to just do a quick body scan. Starting at the top of your head down into your jaw, your neck, your shoulders, all the way down your back, through your legs and down into your feet. Assess the areas where there is tension. If you can, relax that area as much as possible. Just like the breathing exercise take as much time as you need to accomplish this task.

Feeling a little bit more relaxed? I hope so. This next part is a little bit more personal. Whether or not you are comfortable engaging in this exercise in a public place or private I do want to let you know that the following questions may be somewhat triggering. Perhaps you're at the beach, or you are enjoying your book at the breakfast table or perhaps sitting at your gate waiting for a flight. Regardless of your location I want you to be aware that the following inventory is personal. It is, however, critical to consciously assess the root of our insecurities. Without this assessment, it is like taking a trip without a map. We must see where we've been and to understand whether or not we want to leave an area. When we decide that we want to leave an area, we need a roadmap in order to get where we want to go.

This is your map. We just need to figure out where we are first.

I want you to close your eyes again. Take a deep breath and imagine yourself standing on a stage in front of thousands of people in the audience. You are also being televised. Millions of people are watching you via their televisions and computers. You look around the auditorium.

It's a magnificent space. You can hear the din of thousands of people chattering in the distance. There is a spotlight pointed directly at you. You are alone on this stage and as you are standing there you realize that you can only see the first two rows in the audience.

You look at the front row and the people seated there.

Everyone in the front row is someone you know personally. Some are family members. Some are "friends" or acquaintances. Some may be old school mates and co-workers. Some may be past lovers.

All these people in the front row are judging you harshly.

They are pointing fingers at you and laughing uncontrollably.

Some are sitting there staring at you in judgment and disappointment.

A couple of these people are taking deep breaths of resignation and checking their watches as if their time could be better spent elsewhere.

Who are these people laughing at you?

Can you see their faces clearly? Do you recognize them?

Who is the person sitting in the middle pointing and laughing the hardest at you?

Who is the person in the front row who cannot be bothered to point at you but instead sits there and stares at you with disapproval while they roll their eyes at you?

Who are the rest of the people in the front row enjoying your discomfort?

Now that you have identified the individuals in the front row let's look at the second row of individuals. Keep in mind that this auditorium houses thousands and thousands of people but you are only able to see the people in the first two rows. These are the people that are the closest to you in your life. These are the people who hold space around you regardless of whether they are loving or toxic in their behaviors towards you.

Take another deep breath.

Ready?

As you scan the second row of people in the audience you see them smiling at you with approval. Many of them are clapping and cheering. As you purposely move from the left to the right you recognize several faces. These are your cheerleaders in your life. You start to feel your shoulders relax. Several of them are holding a thumbs up. A couple are holding up signs with your name and a heart. The rest of them are chanting your name in support. Your heart returns to a normal rhythm.

When you look at the second row of people who is the person who is clapping the hardest?

Which person has tears streaming down their face in unconditional love and affection for you?

Who is shamelessly yelling your name and waving a sign in support of you?

Can you name the rest of the people in the second row?

Now that you have identified the people in the first row as well as the people in the second row you are ready to begin your inventory.

As you stand on stage you can feel the heat of the spotlight. Perhaps you are unsure as to why you are on stage to begin with. Maybe you can remember a time where you were on stage in the past.

What were you feeling and thinking at that time?

If you've never been on stage before, that's OK. As you move through this exercise, simply imagine what you think you would feel.

How would you describe your emotional state?

Are you excited? Are you terrified? Are you numb? Are you fearless?

Do you have something to offer all these people who are gathered in the auditorium?

Why do you think the people are there?

The point of this exercise is to isolate your vulnerabilities. When we imagine ourselves being the center of attention it can be overwhelming for many of us. Often people who have experienced trauma feel unworthy of love.

So why is it so terrifying to be the center of attention?

Let's look at emotional trauma through the lens of a physical injury.

Imagine that at some point in the distant past you are in an accident. For instance, let's say that you are a child and you go on a bicycle ride. As you are riding your bicycle, a dog runs out in front of you causing you to veer off the road and into the ditch below. Now for the sake of this analogy, let's say you broke your leg.

A broken leg is a terribly painful injury and one that requires emergency attention.

Most people understand if you do not seek emergency attention for a broken bone, the injury will not heal correctly.

Imagine instead of seeking emergency attention after breaking your leg, you manage to crawl all the way home. Let's say you attempt to immobilize your leg with whatever materials you find. Perhaps you take some ibuprofen or some acetaminophen to help with the pain. Maybe you use ice packs to help with the swelling. You do not seek out professional help for your injury. Over time, your leg hurts a little less. However, you have a limp since the bone, although now healed, did not get set properly. Now that your leg has not healed correctly, you are not able to participate in the same physical activities as your peers. You can no longer try out for any of the sports teams you are interested in joining and you feel less attractive and, therefore, lose confidence in your ability to socialize or date. You are very insecure because of the way you walk now.

Emotional trauma works in a similar way. If a person is emotionally traumatized and does not have support available immediately, then the person who experienced the trauma will do what they can to ease the painful after affects. Drug and alcohol addictions are but one after effect of emotional trauma. Other outcomes of trauma are dysfunctional thinking errors, low self-esteem resulting in unsatisfying or unhealthy intimate partner relationships, depression, anxiety, and even suicidal ideation. Trauma changes the landscape of how we live our lives in many ways. Trauma can be mitigated through therapy even many years later. Have you ever thought about the similarities between physical therapy and psychotherapy? Both variations of therapy work diligently to break down scar tissue and develop strength and mobility. Both can also be extremely painful, as well.

The good news is, that like the broken leg, emotional trauma can be "reset". It takes time, attention, and hard work through the rehabilitation process, but it can absolutely be accomplished with success. Psychotherapy and physical therapy are both painful processes. However, they are also worthwhile and effective.

The point of this chapter is that we need to know what is broken in order to fix it. A lot of our issues are tied up in shame and shame can be a roadblock to recovery.

As you read through this book, we will collectively pull back the layers of our shame and look inward to better define not only what is wrong and what needs to be fixed, but also how to fix it.

I can sit here all day and tell you that you are a worthwhile human being. It takes absolutely nothing away from myself to say that to you. It is the equivalent of lighting a candle from another candle. However, there can be no amount of external validation a person can hear if they do not have the confidence that what they are hearing is the truth. Hopefully, this book will help you reprocess your unhealthy beliefs about yourself and your value as a human being in a healthy way.

So, as you move forward remember this: if you go to a doctor with a limp that resulted from a broken leg many years ago and the doctor says, "We are going to have to do surgery to fix this," you can rightly expect to go through some considerable discomfort. Having surgery on a previous injury is painful. However, the long-term effects of having surgery, as well as physical therapy to strengthen the leg will, theoretically, result in the ability to regain your mobility. Regaining your mobility will not only improve your physical health, but not having the limp and the increased ability to participate in athletic activities will have a significant impact on your feeling of emotional wellness and self-confidence. The same can be said for addressing old emotional traumas. Just like surgery, unpacking a traumatic event or events can feel maddening.

Why would anyone want to investigate or explore traumatic events? Because, in doing so, you gain insight and power over the influence of the trauma. You relearn what you think about yourself through a powerful new and positive lens. You regain a new perspective about what happened to you and, in doing so, the trauma loses power. You realize your value and purpose in a renewed perspective.

Can you imagine living a happy life without being adversely affected by trauma?

When you read through the following chapters, remember the broken leg metaphor. Any emotional trauma that is triggered through your own rehabilitation process can be compared to a strength building exercise in post-surgery physical therapy. It is painful in the moment, but it is necessary for your long-term health and well-being.

All of this is to help better define the process of trauma and how we work from that in both healthy (love-based) and unhealthy (fear-based) ways. Naturally, you'd be fearful of riding your bike near the area where you had your accident. That's normal and natural to expect a fear response based upon a trauma. What is unhealthy is not ever getting on your bike again and being angry at all dogs for running in front of your bike. Do you see the difference? Being emotionally traumatized and not having the help of a professional to see you through can result in the creation of fear-based thinking. It's only natural to be fearful of any situation, person or environment that resulted in trauma. However, it becomes problematic when it negatively transitions into a way of thinking that colors your entire world, your relationships, and everyday choices. It robs you of achieving your highest potential. It steals joy.

If you're surrounded by people who have their own traumas, then it's even more likely that they are projecting their own fear-based behaviors upon you which magnifies your own experiences. (Remember the front row in the auditorium?) Think about it logically. Why would anyone invest energy in trying to bring you down or find enjoyment in your failures or discomfort? The only logic behind this is individuals with their own unresolved issues are still human beings seeking a connection. If a person feels "broken", then they will naturally, albeit in a dysfunctional manner, seek out the "brokenness" in others. When they see something in another person that matches how they feel, they feel a sense of connection in the most unhealthy, dysfunctional way. If a "broken" person sees someone else with some level of "brokenness", it tends to satiate the need to have connection. Remember, it never has anything to do with your own value or worthiness. When someone wants to see you fail, it's merely because they want a connection with their own failures.

Take a bow and exit stage right just for now. We will come back to the stage later.

As I've come to realize in doing this work as a helper / healer I have found that my story and my personal narrative and life experiences are not unique. There's a bit of relief in knowing that your own history is like the history of other people who have evolved out of their trauma. All humans crave and need connection with other people. The greatest source of distress is the fear of isolation. My own personal trauma is no different. While it may have been something I wore as a defense mechanism to move through the first half of my life, I have gratefully evolved to the point where it no longer affects me negatively, but instead is repurposed as fuel.

As one of five children, I have had many opportunities in my life to grow and learn past my own trauma. I left home at the age of 20 to join the Air Force and, due to my military obligations, was never afforded an opportunity to cultivate a reciprocal relationship with my parents after that. It's not that I didn't try. However, as the years moved on, it became apparent that my absence created a difficulty in maintaining contact (control; influence) on their part. The relationship that we had existed only due to my effort to maintain it. I spent all my free time traveling all the way to Alabama from my duty station at Kirtland AFB in Albuquerque, New Mexico and back. Those were long, lonely drives across the country. Looking back, I realized that, at the time, I felt that I was obligated to do this. Whether it was implied through my family or culturally speaking, I do remember feeling guilty at the prospect of using my free time to do things that I wanted to do, such as travel to places I had never been or see a concert instead of using that money for gas or airfare to spend minimal time with family. It was a difficult experience to grow through that process and have the feeling that I was not worth enough (my assumption) for my parents to make the effort to reciprocate my efforts. I had expected that my parents would engage and maintain with me in a healthier way. However, looking back through the lens of who I am today, I realize that they did the best they could with all the pressures and responsibilities they had going on. I think they cared as best they could, given their own dynamics, cultural influences, and in particular, my father's own emotional trauma. I realize now the evolution of who I am today is, in part, a direct result of being left to fend for myself in this world. I wouldn't have asked for it at the time, but I am deeply grateful for the experience today, as it provided me with the ability to grow and reach a potential that I'm certain would not be obtained had I never left rural Alabama.

It goes without saying that my experiences in life are vastly different than those of my siblings. To their own credit, through the years, they remained in constant contact with our parents, creating new memories and perhaps having opportunities to work through and let go of these harmful experiences. We all endured in differing but equal ways. Despite my trauma, and through my personal therapeutic growth, I can readily volunteer that I am grateful I was not groomed, out of some sense of loyalty, to adhere to any type of dogma or organized religion. As a child, I felt isolated and alone, as many children of addicts do. I look back now, and I realize that it was a critical dynamic that help me become the person that I am today. I really believe that, had I been in a family where we went to church and where we spent time together and where me and my siblings were not emotionally and physically abused, that we would've held some sense of appreciation and loyalty to our caregivers. That loyalty and appreciation would have, more than likely, caused me to adhere to some sense of religious dogma and or cultural attachment as a measure of connection and commitment to those individuals who sacrificed so much to my care and well-being, as many people often do. This is how religion, social norms, and cultural grooming is handed down from generation to generation. When a person has a healthy sense of belonging to a group, therein lies the implication of adhering to dogma, traditions, rules, and otherwise expectations of behaviors based upon those cultural norms. Children do not choose to become Christian or Muslim or Jewish or whatever because they read about it and decide that is their path in life, typically. People adhere to a faith mainly because of where they are born in the world and who their families are. Is it brain-washing? Is that too strong a statement? One thing is for sure in this book is, that at no point in time, do I want you to feel judged or blamed. You're not wrong. If something you read feels triggering or makes you feel injured or offended, please know that the intention is to provide logical assertion and nothing more. You're a beautiful and loving human being who deserves opportunities to right any wrongs and find peace, love, and joy. This includes your faith, regardless of how you found it.

My statements are not intended to find blame or fault. In fact, it is quite the opposite. They are intended to encourage the reader to understand, think, and feel without any external influence or consequence. While my experiences as a child were predominately dysfunctional and abusive, I'm grateful for my childhood experiences. Because of this, I have been challenged in ways that have brought me to realizing my authentic self and optimal potential. I realize I would not be the person that I am today we're I not afforded the opportunity to think for myself and to decide for myself who and what I wanted to be in my life. I also empathize for the people who feel such an incredible obligation to their caregivers, whether those are parents, grandparents, aunts, and uncles etc., to adhere to a faith and or dogma as a measure of appreciation and respect. I cannot even begin to imagine who I would be today if I had to go to a church and go through the motions of a religion simply because I felt compelled to demonstrate my respect to the people who sacrificed everything in their lives to give me the life I have today. I never felt required to follow any religion as a point of familial obligation and for that, I am deeply grateful.

When we talk about fear-based thinking, it often comes from a deeply injured sense of self. Human development theorists attest that our personalities are developed from our earliest experiences. Even infants, without having developed a language ability, will derive a sense of fear based upon implicit experiences. If a baby is lying in their crib with a wet diaper, diaper rash, hungry and is hearing screaming in the next room, the child will develop a basic sense of lack of safety. The child who has his/her diaper tended to and has no discomfort from a diaper rash and who is nursed by his/her mother with calm and direct eye contact, will experience a calming sense of safety. The fear-based thinking model starts very early and, without mitigation or a timely interruption of fear-based events, will cultivate a sense of fear based emotional response to their environment as they grow into adulthood. Even newborn babies are born with an implicit sense of fear. Studies have shown babies respond to conditions in their environments, whether those are fearful or safe and loving. Cortisol in the body that is triggered by a fear response in the baby, cultivates a lifelong foundation for baseline anxiety, something many of my clients deal with daily.

While my childhood was consistently fear-based, I did experience love occasionally and had the safety of this in the relationship I had with my grandparents, as well as my parents on rare occasion. My tender childhood friendships were a glimpse of a love emotion that I was untrusting of throughout my adolescence and early adulthood. Fear was predominating and consistent, therefore I did not trust love when it showed up. As a result, I grew up a very angry child that turned into a very angry teenager and adolescent and young adult. Fortunately, or unfortunately depending upon your perspective, I learned to use that anger and passion in unhealthy ways to mitigate any fear. I would be remiss if I did not express my gratitude for my experiences. While I would never recommend my experiences as a child to anyone, I would recommend isolating the things to be grateful for as a measure of personal growth. I would not be writing this book were it not for those adverse experiences during my childhood. I know and understand pain as a child, and I empathize with anyone who experienced pain and trauma. No child should ever feel discouraged, discarded, used, abused, worthless, hated, or in the way. No child should ever feel fear as their consistent emotional state of being. Every child is born with a purpose and, as a result, every person has a purpose.

I choose to use my experiences with trauma as fuel and motivation to explore and evolve in this world on my terms. It has been incredibly empowering through my journey and my hope is that it will have a lasting positive effect for you as well.

Hopefully this will help you understand some things about yourself and the dynamics you've been existing in. Perhaps this book will give you the courage to start making some necessary changes in your own life. You cannot expect to take a shower and get clean, and stay clean, if you're consistently jumping into mud. You must stop jumping into the mud in order to have consistency in staying reasonably clean. You can go to therapy every day of the week, but if you are leaving your therapist's office and going home to an abusive partner, a toxic work environment, or dealing with an abusive family member, then you are not making necessary changes to remove yourself from these environments in a healthy and safe way.

Bear in mind that I fully appreciate how leaving an abusive relationship can be unsafe for the partner and any children involved. Conduct an internet search for local support groups and safe houses to help you leave an abusive partner. There are agencies and organizations all over the country ready and willing to help you and any children leave a dangerous situation. Please contact these organizations before planning to leave a violent partner.

Chapter Three: Clutter goes into more detail on this topic. You can go to therapy for the rest of your life, but it's not going to do a damn thing for you until you cut out these influences. I have an intimate understanding and a keen appreciation of how difficult it is to remove toxic influences in your life. My hope for you in reading this book is that you will start to see that spark and that willingness to regain, or to gain for the first time ever, your own sense of wellbeing and to shut out the individuals who are using you and your energy to prop themselves up in their own toxic existence. I'm talking about those people who are so beat down themselves that they must put you down in order to make themselves feel better.

We are going to talk about self-respect, love of self, and the intolerance of toxic behavior from other people. We are going to talk about the difference between people you genuinely care about who are going through a rough time and who need your friendship, compassion, and love versus individuals who are parasitic and siphoning off your precious fuel as their own. We are going to talk about doing the work of repairing your own psyche and we are going to talk about any damages that you've caused to other people. We will talk about accountability and making those wrongs right. We will do this without any sort of deprecation of self because there is no deprecation to be had. You are a worthy and loving and valuable person. Because of this, you are accountable for your behavior and your treatment of other people. You are accountable for your own energy and how that energy is utilized. You are responsible for your own recovery and for growing and evolving and for setting a healthy and functional example if you have children. You deserve to be inspired by others and that makes you responsible to inspire other people. **Flip!** is written to inspire you and people like you who have a need to understand their pain and where it comes from in a logical sense. In doing so, you can see how to remove your emotional response to trauma and see your negative experiences logically.

When you do this, it is just as simple as changing the channel on the tv or radio. You can choose to change your thinking. You can learn how to respond to your environment in love instead of fear. Can you imagine?

CHAPTER TWO

JUDGMENT

When we look at other people we don't know and have never met before, we often formulate opinions about them, whether they are conscious or subconscious. We all do this. It's part of our evolutionary need to survive. The caveman part of us needs to seek those that are familiar and that can be trusted and avoid those that are unfamiliar or different. Anyone that appears or acts in a manner that is foreign to us will naturally be suspect. It doesn't mean that you're going to suspect every stranger you meet as a potential enemy. It means when we see people who live their lives differently than we do, we tend to pay more attention. We observe them more consciously. It's a curious thing to meet someone who is comfortable in their different attitudes, values, and ideals. We observe differences because it is simply ingrained in our biology to do so. Often, culture dictates that this is a flaw of our character and something to be avoided. Socially speaking, it is inappropriate to place judgment upon those who look differently, act differently, pray differently, or dress differently than we do. However, we still do it as a measure of curiosity and comparison. Going a little deeper, if a person is already insecure about who they are in the world, meeting a person who is quite different in appearance, particularly if that person gives off an air of confidence, can make the insecure person feel threatened. If we are in a clan of cavemen and we see someone from a different clan approach us, we would naturally be on guard because we would need to protect our food stores and shelter. We would naturally be suspect of anyone coming towards our clan because food and shelter are a rare commodity for the caveman, so we must survive and that means by confronting strange clans that are foreign to us. Of course, this is not a justification for bias or stereotypes, but more of a logical and foundational explanation why some of those factors exist to begin with.

That need for survival is still deeply ingrained in our brain. Contemporary culture is consistent in reminding us of how we are not cavemen and how outdated the construct of bias and judgment is. The difference between bias or other discrimination is having a deeply rooted sense of judgment of those who appear strange to us is vastly different than allowing that judgment to metastasize into hateful behavior and dehumanizing treatment of others. Research has shown that individuals who adhere to these biases and stereotypes about people who look and act differently than themselves, is indicative of lower intelligence, lower educational levels and a profound lack of diversity and positive exposure to differing cultural influences. It makes sense if you consider that anyone who hasn't traveled the world would be more likely to be on guard around a foreigner than someone who's an experienced world traveler and has had the opportunity to learn about many different cultures than his or her own. In fact, because we know consciously that society does not approve of us placing judgment on those that are different to us that we have naturally become deeply reserved in admitting our bias. It's ironic that sometimes we fear being judged so we hide our own judgments because we are told that they are wrong. That said, a key element to evolving, growing and healing is to take an honest assessment of personal bias. Once that has been identified then you can further investigate where that notion comes from and whether or not it is something you want to hold on to as a measure of personal growth and evolution. If a child is raised by a parent who believes that women are not as smart as men, then logically, the child will more likely adopt this assertion or some aspect of it. Have you ever known someone who acted in a way that indicated their own personal bias towards someone else? Perhaps you knew a neighbor at one time who didn't care for a particular family when they moved into the neighborhood. It's important to address these beliefs during the evolution of personal change. Once we adopt a sense of equanimity toward others, we will be able to let go of unhealthy ideals and limits to our personal potential.

Why is there a topic on judgment and personal bias in a book that is supposed to be about wellness and healing? Because in order to heal and grow, we must fully account for our bias in this world. Again, not a place of judgment or blame, but if you have a predisposed opinion of other people based upon a cultural dynamic, then you cannot fully grow and heal without taking inventory of where that belief came from. Bear in mind there is a fundamental difference between being aware of differences versus allowing those differences to evolve into unhealthy bias. You can be aware that your neighbors pray on Friday or don't eat meat without bearing ill will towards them because of it. If you do have ill will toward someone that you don't know, we will address that too. It's important to be aware of how fear and the thinking that evolves from that manifests in our lives in a dysfunctional way. We will explore deeper and more precise aspects of this behavior in the following chapters on Culture and Worthiness.

Before you can grow, you must heal. Before you can heal, you must understand what is broken. When you take inventory of dysfunctional opinions, beliefs, and cognitions you can accurately identify what part needs to change.

Here is a test: Consider the following statement:

"All human beings are born equal. There is no race, religion, birthright, sexuality, intellect, or ability that makes any one person "better" or more "worthy" than another person. The most destitute individual conceived in incest, rape, etc. is worth just as much as a child born into royalty with all the titles and distinctions implied."

Do you agree with this statement? If not, why? This is the beginning of your journey. We are all spiritual beings having a human experience. You may ask yourself why this is important to your own personal growth. It is critical to understand that when we equal ourselves to one another, we become empowered by understanding and empathy. When we understand we may have been culturally influenced to believe that a group of people are considered "less than" the group we belong to, then we can learn to let go of old programming and adopt new healthy belief systems that foster our own healing. Additionally, if you are of the opinion that you belong to a sub-set of people or group that feels marginalized or discriminated against, you can make an observation of the error in that thought process and learn to start letting it go and living up to your own fullest potential with the newfound knowledge that you're equal and worthy to every other person, despite what other people may tell you from their own fear-based mindset.

The challenge in all of this is to educate ourselves and to be aware of what our physiological responses to threats are. While we can access all forms of modern communication, education, and enlightenment, we are still a product of evolution. This plays out so many ways in our lives. It's key to understand why we feel the way we do when we see someone who looks differently than we do. When we understand this, we do better, we feel better, and we act better.

Several years ago, I was working out in a gym during one of our many military transitions.

We were living temporarily in the base hotel. I was unfamiliar with the base gym I was utilizing and was a bit anxious about working out around people that I didn't know. My heightened sense of awareness and heightened expectation of judgment from others put me into a position of the "best defense is a good offense" mentality. I honestly didn't think of it at the time, but looking back, I can see clearly how judgmental I was feeling in the moment. I also can clearly see the reason for all that judgment was because I was in fear of being judged. This was the first time I had attended this gym. I approached the front door and determined I was not comfortable asking any questions about the gym, where the locker rooms were, where the cardio and weight rooms were. I presented my identification and took a gym towel. As I walked in through the gym, I attempted to investigate each room as though I was looking for someone and not trying to figure out where the recumbent bicycles were. If anyone asked me if they could help me, I was prepared to tell them I was looking for my then husband. They wouldn't be able to help me and, theoretically, leave me be. There was something terribly triggering about being an Air Force veteran married to an active duty Army soldier walking through a Marine Corps gym. I felt a bit on edge, as I did not want to seem weak or unintelligent. The gym was covered with extremely fit young men and, while that may sound exciting to many, I can assure you I was not in that frame of mind. I felt physically inferior and the fact that I did not see but a few other women (who appeared just as fit, if not more so than their male counterparts) made me feel even more isolated. "What am I doing here? I could just do a workout back in the hotel room," I thought to myself. I continued to inspect each room as I approached. The gym wasn't that big, and I wasn't stupid. I could figure this out on my own and I didn't need some jock feeling as though he was rescuing me. I was irritated by the time I located the massive cardio room with its expansive row of treadmills, stair climbers and bicycles. I surveyed the room briefly and isolated what I thought was the safest piece of equipment based upon its location in comparison to the other individuals in the gym. As I took my position on one of the recumbent bicycles, I adjusted the length of the stirrups after giving the equipment a thorough scrubbing with the provided spray and wipes. Truthfully, I wasn't really concerned about the machine being unsanitary as much as I was interested in putting on a display of concern about the sanitation. If anyone was watching me, they would see me taking the time to preserve my

own wellness. Sort of a demonstration of my need to proj-
ect an air of heightened social positioning to anyone who
may have been watching me. Basically, the equivalent of
chest pounding to show domination. (I was still wonder-
ing what I was doing here.) Also, the recumbent bike, as
you may know, is the perfect piece of equipment to allow
you to fully extend and contract the leg muscles all while
being completely distracted with the use of a smart phone
and social media. So, as I got settled in and started the
repetition, I opened my social media app and proceeded
to scroll through the myriad of posts with the intention of
securing my anxious mind with a welcome distraction.
My intention was to appear as relaxed as possible in my
perusal of social media. However, I was overly aware of
my situation and was on heightened alert with regards
to the location of each gym attendee. After several min-
utes of scrolling through the mindless jargon, a woman
climbed into the saddle at the seat directly adjacent to me.
This is not normally an issue however I took some mild
offense to the fact that there was an entire row of recum-
bent bicycles available for her use and yet she chose the
one directly beside me. I felt irritated and annoyed with
her selection. Did she not understand the social rules?
If you use a public restroom and there is a long row of

vacant toilets available and only one person is using a toilet at that time, social rules dictate that you do not select the toilet directly next to the occupied one. (My mind was racing. You just don't do that! What is her damn problem?) Everyone knows these social rules extend to other situations, much like utilizing available exercise equipment in the gym. Like in the restroom scenario, nobody wants to hear your business going on next-door to you, just like you don't want to smell the person who is working out next to you or hear the grunting or heavy breathing during their exertion. So many rules were being broken. My heart rate increased due more to my social anxiety than the exertion of the machine. Obviously, if the restroom (or the gym in this case) is completely packed, then naturally the social rules don't apply because you can't help but to select the only available piece of equipment or the remaining available toilet. But no, she had to pick the one directly next to me. My anxiety shot through the roof at that moment. I felt flush and my heart rate was much higher than it should've been at that moment, given my physical exertion. Was she pranking me? Were there other people in the gym watching this? The idea of this infuriated me. Who the hell did she think she was? I would have discontinued my workout and returned to our hotel room but then that would mean she won. They all would win, and I couldn't allow that to happen. I had to keep working out and pretend her presence was not an issue for me. Just over here minding my business and checking out my friend's social media posts. My mind explored a variety of different hostile options. How dare she? How dare she come into my space when there's so much other available equipment that she could utilize? Hell, at this point I couldn't even concentrate on my work out. I couldn't even concentrate on my social media. I was growing more and more enraged by the second. What do I do? Do I confront her? Do I ask her what her problem is? God no, that could backfire immensely. She was an older lady and, granted while yes, there are women in the military, I was more concerned with the fact that she might be the spouse of some high-ranking base official. I didn't care if she didn't like me, I certainly could not put my husband's career in a chokehold like that, through my adverse behavior. However, the nature of my char-acter did not allow me to ignore this behavior. I had to do something. So, what do I do? I turn the flash off my camera on my phone and take a couple of test photos of my feet to ensure that it was indeed shut off. And, at the right moment, I took a couple photos of the back of her head that also incorporated a slice of my own position so that the viewer could clearly see we were situated next to each other. Once the photograph was posted to my social media, I proceeded to vomit a toxic rant of injustice based upon her choices of equipment. As soon as I began my dialogue I started to relax and feel better, knowing that the rest of my "clan" would validate my feelings and back me up. I needed their approval. I needed them to tell me that my rage and vitriol was appropriate and how dare she choose that piece of equipment so close to me and interrupt my work out. I posted it and waited. Over the next several hours I received a couple of validating and encouraging comments that basically told me that my judgment of this woman was valid. Looking back now though, I see with some clarity that had any of my (clan) friends on social media countered my opinions with logic and an opposing suggestion of an opinion, I would've been terribly offended. That's not what friends do. Friends support each other no matter what, right?

Today, thinking back on that event, I am not ashamed about my behavior. While my thinking was not correct, I must give myself space and understanding as to why I reacted the way that I did. I didn't know that woman. I did know that I was uncomfortable in an unfamiliar gym around people I did not know. I was full of anxiety from walking around the gym trying to navigate where the weight room was versus the Nautilus versus the cardio, etc. I know my personality enough to know that, given enough time, I will find exactly what I need to find. However, being a woman on a military installation, it is virtually guaranteed that if you walk around the gym looking for a workout area, you will almost always be approached by someone with good intentions attempting to help you navigate. It does not bother me to do reconnaissance. While we were staying in this area of the base for another week or two, I needed to be familiar with the gym anyway, so I gave myself a tour, all the while expecting some young pumped up servicemember to approach me and try to make themselves feel better about helping the older lady find what she's looking for. It has always been about my trepidation with my own anger and my fear of behaving inappropriately, that would backfire on my husband. (For those of you unfamiliar with this concept, in the military, all servicemembers are held equally responsible for the behavior of their dependents. If I were to throw a fit in the gym, I would have been removed and my husband would have been punished for my behavior.) I look back upon that day and realize, by the time I had located my equipment, I had already formulated my opinion about everyone in the gym. This was even though no one had attempted to instruct me on where the "little ladies go" to do their "little lady work outs". This is all subconscious and was not something I was consciously considering. In fact, it was such a norm for me to be at such a heightened space of anxiety, it would've never occurred to me to take a breath and consciously lower into a calmer headspace. I was merely in survival mode. I was very aware I was in a foreign environment around people that were not of my "clan". My caveman responses were extremely triggered. I was navigating unknown territory and needed to be especially defensive. In my case, being defensive means to be offensive. The poor lady who parked her carcass next to me in the gym that day was probably scared too, now that I think about it. She might've felt more comfortable being next to another woman as opposed to the other beef heads running around. She was older and she was by herself. From a physical agility standpoint, she offered absolutely no threat whatsoever. It would be easy for me, at this point, to be judgmental of myself when looking back on my behavior, but the lesson here is to refrain from using blame in reviewing our previous behaviors.

We look back, assess, learn, and move on with possession of self and an understanding about how to do better in the future. We do this with kind understanding and a conscious avoidance of deprecation of self. I am a good person now. I was a good person then. I just responded to this situation based upon what I knew to be a good response at the time. I would not respond that way today. I would not post pictures to social media, as that is not a love-based thought process. Changing the channel from fear-based thinking (posting a picture to social media for others to judge) to love-based thinking (mindful awareness of self with deliberate empathy for others) is a life-long process and one that I continue to this day.

Understanding judgment includes understanding the judgment of self as well. We can only do as well as our logic, our experience, and wisdom from our own growth will take us. I was doing the best that I could at that point in my life. I am very happy and grateful that I'm doing better now, but there's absolutely no benefit whatsoever in looking back and judging myself. In fact, thinking back on that situation provides me with a narrative to openly share my own experiences with judgment, both from a fear of judgment as well as an expression of judgment of others.

I must admit, I do catch myself judging others. I'm a human being and there will be people around me that I interact with who are nefarious with their intent. Engaging in fear-based thinking is different from feeling actual fear. There will always be people who will engage in a manner inconsistent with my idea of what is appropriate. There will always be people who violate boundaries. There will always be people who will behave and engage in a way that completely messes with my head (I'm talking about people who park their grocery cart in the middle of the aisle while looking at canned corn on the shelf in the grocery store.) I think the biggest part of my growth regarding judgment is the balance of understanding what is real and what is inferred. There is a difference between a person who is behaving rudely versus someone who is following you through the store. Now when I'm in the grocery store, for example, I make a conscious attempt to put my cart as close to the shelf as possible, to ensure I am occupying as small as possible footprint out of respect for other people. I also try to navigate in a way that allows other people time to get out of the way without my intentionally seeking to make them feel shame. The problem with this is that I expect the same and that doesn't always happen.

Do you ever feel frustration when other people behave in a manner that is inconsistent with your values? It's frustrating of course, but when we come from a love-based mindset, we aren't as apt to judge. It's the fear-based thinking that takes these events to the next level in our brain. We feel personally affronted as though they are leaving their cart in the middle of the aisle intentionally to cause us distress. Conversely, I can be in the healthiest head space, feeling love and appreciation for my fellow man and still feel fearful when someone is threatening me. It is important to be aware of the difference between the two mindsets.

I'm not trying to say that gymnasiums and grocery stores are inherently flawed places, but let's just say it's a growth opportunity for me to take the initiative and measures of prevention of anxiety prior to entering these types of establishments, (or any forum where my social anxiety will be potentially triggered.) As a person who has battled social anxiety, I am certain I am not alone in feeling hesitation in visiting these environments. I understand I'm going to be emotionally charged in these situations, therefore, I hold an obligation to myself in taking measures to prevent these triggers from affecting me at least as much as I possibly can. What that means for me personally is I meditate prior to engaging, as well as wearing headphones and sunglasses if appropriate. I don't know about you, but I have absolutely no problem with wearing sunglasses in the grocery store. Having lack of eye contact is tremendous in preventing anxiety, at least for me. I can see you, but you can't really see me, and I feel better just talking about it. Bear in mind, this is all about my own expectations of being triggered by the social behaviors of other people and my inherent reaction to judgment. It is still a process for me and one that I take very seriously before entering any social situation.

So, what are your judgments? More importantly what are your judgments about yourself? The key to finding peace and a sense of calm in your heart and your spirit is understanding what the trouble is to begin with. Much of our anxiety is based upon our previous experiences and it becomes a belief about what will potentially happen in the future. As a result, we are mostly judgmental of ourselves first and, therefore, from that position become judgmental of other people. So again, when you look at yourself, what do you see?

When you look inside your heart, what do you see?

Do you see a good person?

Do you see a harmful person?

Do you see a good person that maybe does some harmful behaviors from time to time?

We can dig a little deeper and even go so far as to say, "Do I deserve to feel better about myself?" If you believe that you deserve better, then I applaud you because you are ahead of the curve already. However, if you're reading this right now and you feel isolated and alone and unique in your invalidity, then I can most definitely tell you that this is targeted to you. I firmly believe that no matter who you are, what you are guilty of, how much pain you've caused other people, or what type of insult, tragedy, or trauma you experienced in your life, there is recovery and a sense of newness for you. You do not have to be judged by yourself or others in order to isolate some sensibility of worthiness. You're already worthy. It's not an easy path but it is a worthwhile one. You only must believe that you deserve better and that you're willing to do the hard work to make positive changes, including taking ownership of your mistakes.

A big part of this recovery process in isolating your own internalized judgment is to figure out what you're judging yourself for. Is it a learned behavior? Did you grow up watching a loved one behave in the same manner? Much like how children learn to speak a language, we also learn behaviors. Just like learning a new language, you can also learn new ways of thinking and behaving. Are your learned behaviors something that you should address as a measure of your own healing?

If you've made mistakes no matter how big and how huge and how large those mistakes are you can recover. (This is the part where clients will ask about people on death row and those who have been guilty of the most egregious offenses you can imagine.)

The truth with people who have committed the most heinous offenses you can imagine, is they are just as capable as anyone else of taking accountability and ownership of their behaviors. I will say many of the people who commit terrible crimes also have preexisting mental health conditions that remove them from a sense of reality and, as such, remove any willful capability or intent to take responsibility for their actions. Often, they have no conscious ability or intent to recover. This is a generalization, however. Barring those individuals, if a person has committed an offense they want to accept responsibility for, then yes, they can. It's important to understand that for a person who has committed a murder, for instance, taking accountability doesn't make the offense go away. Nor does it remove the pain that offense caused to the loved ones of the victim. We are talking about personal growth and healing. There can be little done to ease the suffering of a crime such as this and I want to be clear the intent of this practice is to understand that. On the outset, virtually nothing will change except for how the offender feels about him or herself. Hopefully, if you're reading this, you're able to see with some perspective that accountability and ownership begins with yourself and doesn't involve self-shaming or judgmental behaviors.

Isolating your judgment of self is key to understanding why you made those mistakes to begin with. You may think what you've done in the past is so profound and so harmful and so hurtful that you cannot work past it. I have worked with people who have committed the most heinous and egregious acts and I can tell you that when you take authentic ownership of the harm you have inflicted and accept accountability for your errors, your mistakes, and the inflicted trauma upon other people, that is when you start to let go and that is when you start to grow. It goes without saying this is the hardest part of self-discovery and one of which many people simply cannot overcome. For some, it's too heavy to allow the responsibility to ignite the shame within. Instead, they opt to deny any culpability in offenses they have committed and choose, instead, to delude themselves into an alternate state of reality. Sometimes the alternate state is more comfortable than allowing themselves to see reality for what it truly is and, as such, being present in their own accountability. People who have harmed others or who have allowed harm to come to others may not believe they are worthy of being whole and living a life of happiness and fulfilment. That is where being non-judgmental is critical to recovery.

Additionally, moving through this process incorporates an understanding that, while you may be able to attain a feeling of wellness, those whom you have harmed in the past may continue to project the pain they feel as a result of your actions. There's nothing you can do about this except to understand it for what it is and respect the outcome without allowing it to degrade your healing. You cannot always affect change in the hearts of others. However, when you accept accountability and take ownership often it results in a diffusion of these projections from those you've harmed. Likewise, if you're projecting your pain upon others for their transgressions, it's often the result of their unwillingness to hold space for their responsibility to you. As you read through these chapters you will start to better understand the dynamics that created your mindset. From this you will begin to understand how to disentangle yourself from fear-based thinking.

It is critical to understand that in doing this work, you do so for your own growth and healing. The purpose of embarking on this wellness journey has nothing to do with how other people view you, particularly when those are people that you've harmed in the past. Being accountable to your mistakes, offenses, and even crimes does not guarantee forgiveness from others. In fact, you should move forward in healing fully expecting those who harbor hostility and resentment towards you for your actions to continue doing so.

Take accountability anyway. (See chapter on Accountability)

The first step, however, is getting to the point where you believe you deserve to grow. People who have made many mistakes in life, that have hurt other people, may have internalized their own accountability and as a result, marked it with shame and a belief they do not deserve good things.

A few years, back I had a client named Paul (not his real name of course) who was 10 years sober and wanted to speak with me about his relationships with his adult children. Paul was fit, well-groomed, and articulate. He did not present as the kind of person you'd assume had been a lifelong alcoholic. (What do alcoholics look like anyway?) Paul had tried many times to connect with his adult twin daughters, but was rebuffed, though 'in a kind way' he reassured me. I knew that this troubled

Paul and I asked him to tell me more about their relationship. He explained to me that, after high school, they both went to college, "which I paid for," he quipped. The girls never wanted to come home and spend time with Paul and his new girlfriend, now wife, at the time. He expressed to me that he'd done "everything he was supposed to do" to "make it up to the girls" for everything that happened when they were little. We talked about Paul's history with alcohol and, while he readily admits to what he can remember, he expressed shame about the things that happened when he blacked out. I asked Paul, "What is it that you want in regard to having a relationship with your daughters?" "I just want to be there for them," Paul replied. "So, what's stopping you from being there for them, then?" Paul gazed out the window with tear filled eyes and said, "I guess I just want them to forgive me." "What makes you think they haven't?" "I don't know. But neither one wants me at the house, and they won't let me see my grandkids without them or their husbands' present. I'd like to spend time with my grandkids without having to be supervised. I feel like they are punishing me" "Do you think that you've earned that, Paul?" He looked at me with a surprised expression. "I'm sober. I've been sober for years. None of that stuff is going to happen again." "That's not what I asked, Paul." In a slightly offended tone, he responded "What are you talking about?" "I mean do you think that just because you're sober now, your daughters have forgotten how you behaved when they were little? Do you think they are trying to judge you and punish you for the past by keeping your grandkids away from you or do you think they are being good parents by making sure their children are safe? Don't you think your daughters have a right to feel the way they do in maintaining safety with their children around you? Paul, you admitted it yourself, you were very violent when you would drink, and you even went to jail for domestic violence toward your ex-wife. Don't you think your daughters are simply being good mothers?" Paul fidgeted in his seat for a minute. "You're absolutely right. I'm a complete sack of shit." "Paul, I didn't say that, and you know it. I take offense to your posture towards me right now. It's inappropriate. Don't put words into my mouth. Just answer the question." "I'm so sorry. That was wrong of me. I apologize. It's just I'm so hurt, and I don't know what to do. I feel like I'm being punished for something that I cannot make right."

Paul and I continued to have many sessions afterwards and he slowly began to understand where his daughters were coming from with regards to his visits with their families and especially with regard to spending time with his grandchildren.

Paul showed up early for an appointment many months later. "I talked with both of my daughters. Their husbands were there, too. I told them I'd been talking with you and you helped me understand what they had to deal with regarding my drinking when they were little girls. I told them I was deeply sorry for all the pain I caused them and the pain I caused their mother. I told them I understood why they didn't want to leave their children alone with me. I told them I am proud of them for being good parents and while I know I would never harm any of my grandkids, I respect their wishes and understand why they feel the way that they do." Paul was openly tearful and grabbed a tissue from the box to wipe his eyes and nose. "They started crying. I even got a hug from both of my daughters. It was the first time in a long time I felt ok." Paul took a breath and hung his head. "I drank to avoid the pain of my father's abuse. He was an awful, mean tyrant who broke my jaw when I was

11, after I tried to defend my mother from his wrath. He was known in town as the drunk. He couldn't keep a job and the only money we had came from the ironing and sewing my mother would do. It was all she could do to keep her head up. She was exhausted morning, noon, and night. My father would get drunk, accuse her of cheating, and would spend hours beating her. "When was she going to cheat?" he stated in feigned sarcasm. "She was his slave from sunrise to sunset. She never left the damn house!" Paul's tears had dried at this point, as he gazed out of my office window. "My father was a drunk and awful and I turned out to be just like him, at least for a while." He broke his gaze from the window and looked at me "I'm not awful. I'm not a drunk. I'm a good person who hurt the people I care about. I know they have forgiven me years ago and now I'm ready to forgive myself. I don't want to carry this burden anymore."

Paul married his girlfriend and, in his vows, promised to always take good care of himself for her. His daughters also attended his wedding. Paul remains sober to this day.

Paul's journey is not that unusual. Many people experience domestic violence and drug and alcohol abuse within the home to grave results. Many people are traumatized from having had to deal with the outbursts from the traumatized alcoholic. Children often internalize these experiences as having been their fault and thus the cycle continues. Paul's recovery is one that posits an example of what psychotherapy and good old fashion hard work can do in isolating the logical cause of harm. When we remove shame, blame, and self-judgment, miracles can and do happen!

Paul's evolution began simply because he was able to see his worth. He was able and willing to do the work to recover, not only from his own childhood trauma, but to grow from accepting accountability for the harm he caused his own family. He was able to do this by isolating his judgment of himself. He grew up feeling worthless and broken so, therefore, he believed that about himself. His judgments of himself created the template for his abusive and neglectful behavior, especially when he was drinking.

Perhaps your narrative is different from Paul's. However, if you have anything that you need to grow and recover from, the question is do you believe that you deserve to?

Do your judgments of others keep you from growing and healing? Do you judge yourself harshly? Do you hold bias, views, and opinions of yourself that act as roadblocks to your own wellness?

Think about these questions as you read on.

CHAPTER THREE

CLUTTER

We talk all the time about clutter in our home, on our desk at work, in our car, or in our purse. etc. It is not common that we discuss the clutter in our minds, in our lives, and in our hearts, and in our spirit. However, it is vital that we address the clutter we all collect over the years and in doing so, how it drains our energy and distracts us from focusing on the things that are functional and healthy to us. It is no wonder that we feel more relaxed, focused, and in control of our lives when the things that are important to us are managed well, organized, and are not out of place. Energy, stressors, and the projected influences from those in our lives can often become emotional clutter in our hearts much like random items scattered about in our homes. Additionally, we find ourselves discarding items in our home when we inventory their relevance and importance. It should be no surprise when we do a similar inventory on our emotional influences, we learn to bag up and cart off negative and irrelevant stressors as well.

There are all kinds of clutter, in every capacity and in every variety that you could possibly imagine, that occupies space within our lives and our hearts ,rent free. Some of that clutter comes in the form of friendships, family relationships, poor financial management, and our inability to say no to the intrusions of other people, for example. There is virtually no limit to the way clutter can infiltrate our lives. Let's explore this analogy, for instance. Let's pretend that you are covered in dirt from head to toe. You have grime, oil, mud, and dust in your hair and all over your body. You have been covered in this dirt for years. Let's imagine that you have finally decided to rid yourself of all dirt on your body. That's a great choice to make because who doesn't like to be clean? So, let's imagine that in this process you have chosen to prepare your shower by making sure that you have all the necessary soaps, shampoos, conditioners; loofahs, and washcloths you need in order to have a successful shower and to successfully remove all of the dirt and grime from the top of your head to the tip of your toes. You've made sure you have clean towels ready once you step out of the shower. Now that you have taken the time and made the energy investment in turning on the water and getting it to the right temperature, you step inside and it feels wonderful. You look down in the shower you see the grime falling off your body and running into the drain. You let the warm water completely soak your head, you use shampoo that smells wonderful, and you lather up your hair, and you wash your head carefully with kindness and love for yourself. It makes you feel wonderful. You rinse out your hair, you put the conditioner in, and you make sure that you run it through all your hair to ensure that it does its job efficiently and effectively. While you are conditioning your hair, you take your loofah and you put the lavender scented body wash on it, you are getting it soapy and bubbly and lathered up and you start from the ears all the way down to the bottom of your feet, scrubbing away all the years of grime and all the years of dirt and grease and dust, and rinsing it off of your body into the drain. Once you've removed all the dirt, you take time, care, concern, and love for yourself to ensure you have fully rinsed all the soap and every bit of any remaining debris off your body. Next, you're standing there in the shower, squeaky clean, ready for your towels. You step out of the shower, you grab a fluffy clean, white towel, and you start to dry yourself off. You take the other fluffy white towel and wrap it carefully and with love around your head so that it can absorb the remaining water out of your hair. Then you stand there and after all of your effort, after all of the time and energy and money you invested in preparing your shower and getting yourself squeaky clean, you look around your room and realize that it is full of the very grime, dirt, grease, and filth you just took off of your body. What do you think will happen if you continue to live in this type of environment, with all this clutter, dirt, and grime around you? Don't you think if you invest so much time and energy taking care of your body, that you should prevent your body from getting that dirty again? If you allow that type of dirt, grime, and clutter to be manifest in the environment that you exist in regularly, then it only makes sense that the clutter and the dirt that you live in will only naturally get on your body once again.

How does it make you feel to be clean?

How does it feel to look around at your environment? Are you tired of living this way?

The point is, you can get all the therapy in the world to take care of what is going on in your head and your heart, but until you start doing the hard work in your life and categorically making command decisions on what you will and will not tolerate to have an influence on you and your family, then you will continue to be triggered and you will continue to have the lasting effects of trauma due to the exposure of being around the very clutter that you need to remove from your life. Showering will have a limited affect if you are living in squalor. Therapy is only as effective as the changes you are willing to make.

Perhaps you look around and you think "Well, yes ,it does appear to be clutter from the outsider's perspective, but there are things here that I need. I need these papers and I need this tool and I need this piece of decor that I've never managed to use and, oh, by the way, I need this piece of sporting equipment, etc. I just haven't had the time to put it away in a proper storage area. So, I can't get rid of this clutter I just need to organize it."

Much like our personal lives and our professional lives, our homes often reflect what is going on in our heart and our mind. If your home is cluttered, chances are, you've got some questionable boundaries with regards to the things you focus your energy on in your mind. Of course, it's understandable to know that thinking about organizing can be an insurmountable and overwhelmingly stressful concept. If it were easy, people would be neat and tidy all the time.

It's important to take inventory of what is affecting us. Everyone is different. We all have different levels of tolerance with regards to clutter. Clutter doesn't bother some people. In fact, I've met many people who say that they feel comforted with having lots of things lying about in disarray. Much like a nest gives a small mammal comfort and warmth, clutter can do the same for some people. The question is, does the clutter cause stress? If the clutter causes stress, then there needs to be mitigation of that stress. Does the idea of removing the clutter cause stress because you believe that the removal will cause other people stress, so therefore why bother?

Do you live in a nest because your partner likes it that way? Is there a middle ground you can agree to in order to organize the clutter?

Is there filth around you? Do you need help to clean it up?

The main purpose of this exercise is to determine what is causing you stress and to mitigate that in a healthy and productive way. Sometimes the removal of clutter can create stressful dynamics with loved ones. If that is the case, then perhaps a conversation about an agreed upon resolution would be appropriate. The important thing to remember here is to understand what needs to change and to make a concerted healthy effort to do so.

Identifying what is "clutter".

What is cluttering up your psyche? In other words, what is causing you stress? Is this something that you could, in theory, address? For example, if a loved one has received a dire medical diagnosis, then clearly that would result in stress. There is not a whole lot that you can do to mitigate this kind of stress, beyond meditation or prayer and ensuring that you are doing everything you can to be supportive. Take this and compare it to, perhaps, dealing with an in-law or toxic coworker who does not respect personal boundaries. Perhaps you have the parents of your spouse or partner showing up at your home, unannounced, on a regular basis. Would this be a cause of stress that you could mitigate? Does it make you uncomfortable to think about addressing the dynamics of these influences? Perhaps a toxic co-worker expects you to handle part of their workload and functions in a disrespectful manner with regards to your workspace. Are you comfortable addressing your frustration to your boss? Sometimes we are faced with the difficult decision of the enforcement of boundaries with individuals who refuse to acknowledge and respect our space. It often results in a defensive posture from the offender. On the surface, it seems difficult, but quite honestly, it can be a simple fix once you feel confident in the tools that you use to mitigate this strife. Having that type of a situation can be clutter in your mind that is occupying space. Think about it. The things you worry about that you could potentially do something about; don't you feel that you could invest that energy into something more worthy? For many people, it seems easier to "let it go" as opposed to confronting the issue. The fact is, "letting it go" translates into tolerance of the offending behavior and therefore, allowing it to continue. The result is built up stress that has nowhere to go, so it piles up in your head and heart, occupying space and expending your emotional resources in dysfunctional ways.

Identifying clutter and taking action to make necessary changes might not seem like a simple way to navigate this world, however, once you've accomplished this, it will result in fewer stressors. In this case, less is most definitely more.

Remember that removing clutter is critical to the long-term success in your journey to wellness. There are no number of showers you can take that will prevent you from being affected by the clutter in your environment. The same applies to your mental health. In order to preserve all the hard work you have done towards regrouping, rethinking, and re-learning who and what you are in the world, you must address those external influences that consistently erode your positive efforts to wellness.

It's time to break the cycle. It doesn't have to be a heated argument. You can and should address issues that affect your ability to do your job, live in your home, and have your boundaries respected. It's ok if you are unsure of how this should take place.

Talk to your co-worker. Ask them to understand you're trying to work and you don't feel it's fair for you to complete a task. If that doesn't work, talk to your boss. If your boss doesn't help you, perhaps it's time to start looking for other opportunities. If you don't feel like there are other opportunities for you, then maybe start looking at going back to school. Maybe taking some classes or training will empower you to have more choices. Remember, this is all about your own personal growth and ,while it may seem a stretch to consider the dealings of a rude coworker to quitting your job, it is all interconnected to your long-term wellness and happiness. Pay attention to the little things. The clutter in your home caused by poor organizational habits of your partner can trigger other issues in your relationship. Communicate your willingness to help as well as your need for change. If you are not communicating clearly then you cannot expect others to understand what your needs are.

It's ok when others get defensive. If you're being fair in your assertion, you must remember that you're not responsible for how other people respond. That's something we all inherently fear in our relationships with other people. We naturally don't want to rock the boat, so we avoid. When we avoid, we are denying ourselves the very change we are trying to inhabit in our lives. You're not a bad person for asking others to be accountable. Likewise, you expressing a willingness to be accountable is the very foundation for cultivating healthy dynamics in all your interpersonal relationships. Likewise, if you're the source of the clutter in your world, then change is much easier. Your efforts to make these changes may positively affect others, but ultimately it is up to you to do the work. Sometimes it's easier to make adjustments in our lives regarding clutter when we are looking at our living or workspace. What can you change? What can you donate or discard? Then, when you're ready, you can investigate the clutter in your heart. What are you ready to get rid of? What relationships or connections to other people are dragging you down? Do you find yourself overly invested in the relationships of family members, to a point that it is unhealthy? Are you pouring emotional energy into social media? What do you spend your time thinking about and is it healthy?

It is ok to be intimidated by this process because change can be scary. Just remember, change can have tremendous benefits as well.

CHAPTER FOUR

CHANGING

Change is inevitable to growth. It can also be terrifying. Culture teaches us to "commit" to our decisions. "Don't give up." There is implicit shame tied up in quitting a job or getting a divorce, because it's considered "weak" to not stick it out. Something that I have observed, both in my personal life as well as a clinician, is many times people who are the most fearful of change, project that fear on others in the form of shameful judgment. A client of mine was going through a divorce and was on amicable terms with her soon to be ex-husband. Her issue she wanted to discuss with me was dealing with her parents. They had been married for over 40 years. "They hate each other," she told me with a chuckle. "I wish they would have divorced when we were kids. It sure would have made things better for everyone." Her mother thought that she was 'sinning' in divorcing her husband and expressed severe judgment of my client regarding her divorce. "My mother never took the time to seek out an education or explore her own interests. She was too scared to. So, she married my father and made his life a living hell. My dad was no saint, mind you. He cheated on my mother throughout the years and you would have thought that my mom appreciated the fact that he made her the victim in the relationship. It's really twisted. I think my mom is jealous of my ability to leave my marriage. I have a successful career and I'm still young enough to find a new relationship if I want to. I think my mom is projecting her own regret upon me for the way her life panned out." I agreed with my client.

The things that we find comfort in are the things that we are most familiar with. If you look around you will notice there are many people who stay in questionable situations, simply because they are familiar. Some folks would argue that the most terrifying thing for anyone to experience is the unknown. It's probably the reason why many of us fear death. It's also a big reason why it is vital to be present in the moment. However, once you've become present in the moment and you've started to do some critical thinking, you will notice there are needs to be met and changes to be made in order for you to attain purpose and fulfillment in healthy and functional ways. I seek and desire to find joy in my life, not just a simple homeostasis and neutrality. Granted, a lot of us exist only to pay bills and stay out of the focus of other people. When you take a moment to think about this, you must ask the question, "Is this really the way I want to live?" So, when you embark upon an adventure of life fulfilling evolution, ultimately you will have to make some necessary changes.

Friends, lovers, jobs, and family situations are all examples of some heavy emotional work that will have to be done in order to live your authentic life. Initiating the first step on this journey, you must acknowledge that the goal is to find your authentic, joy-filled, and purpose driven life. Your joy will undoubtedly offend, terrify, and confuse many people in your life. Much like my client's mother, she projected her own deeply rooted regret for not taking more initiative in her own life and was harshly judging her daughter for doing so. Can you think of anyone in your life who would potentially feel scorn towards you for making changes in your life?

This is totally OK, even though it may not feel that way at first. You may be harshly judged for taking the initiative to find a sense of fulfillment for yourself. Why do people find these actions so counterintuitive? The truth is, many of us feel either unqualified, undeserving, or overall not worth embarking upon this type of an evolution. When we see other people seeking to improve and to actualize themselves in their own spiritual and emotional growth, it can be quite off-putting to the person who does not understand this. Not to judge them, but it is a simple, reaction-based thinking. The only thing you can do in this process is smile and allow them to feel the way they feel. You can send out good energy in a positive sense of gratitude, but part of the evolutionary process is to understand that you cannot accept their energy as your own. My client knew that her mother would be a speedbump in the divorce process, but instead of allowing her mother's judgment to give her pause, she merely refused to accept her negative energy into her emotional head space.

There is a huge amount of willful intent that is necessary to fully embrace your growth and recovery.

When you decide to make some changes in your life, you will undoubtedly notice that your relationships with certain people will start to change. Perhaps you notice you are engaging with these people less and less. You must do your own personal inventory on these relationships to determine what they're worth is to you. Is it more of a drain to you emotionally to maintain and hold space for this person in your life? If so, it might be best to simply cut ties and move forward in your life and your journey, all while wishing them the best. If you've pulled away from this person and they mean something to you, but they simply do not grasp or understand your journey, then perhaps a conversation should take place.

Space is always good. Taking space and time for yourself, particularly in these relationships where you have embedded yourself to a degree of self-involvement that is unhealthy or dysfunctional for you, then perhaps you must have a conversation with these people. Ultimately, if these people are loyal and well-intended, they will understand that you need to regroup and grow. There are relationships that are absolutely worth saving, but at the same time, you must realize that if you are pouring more out of your pitcher into their cup, then you might want to step back and focus on refilling your own pitcher for a while.

The relationships that are an emotional drain are usually the ones that are most contentious, but at the same time, are often the easiest ones to let go of. There's almost always no emotional attachment to these relationships because of their drain on you and your energy. Ironically, the fear of a confrontation is typically the reason these individuals have access to your emotional energy stores, simply because you don't want to have a confrontation.

Did you know there are worse things in the world than getting into a shouting match with someone who doesn't respect you and repeatedly fails to hold space for what you need from the relationship? True, confrontation can be uncomfortable and, socially speaking, is counter-intuitive to any relationship, but sometimes it's unavoidable when enforcing boundaries and refusing to tolerate toxic behaviors.

You have the right to do it anyway.

Making the decision to release individuals from your life is not necessarily a positive experience nor one that you do as a first resort, but once you've exhausted other options and have made the decision, it is one you should do wholeheartedly, with positive intent for them to secure their own place in a positive space in the future. Regardless, whether positive or negative, their response to your actions is irrelevant to your journey. While you may elect to part ways and wish a person good positive energy on their own life journey, you must remember that your goal is to achieve recovery and wellness in your own life without further depleting your energies in parasitic relationships. Let them go when it is time. Only you will be able to determine when that time is. Change like this is difficult, but is often necessary.

Familial relationships are a little trickier to maneuver. There is a cultural implication that because of a blood relation, you are somehow connected to that individual for the duration of your life, regardless of the level of toxicity it brings to your life. While it may seem controversial, it is not necessary to maintain any harmful relationship. The same goes for family relationships that go with friendships that have always been toxic. Perhaps those relationships were not always toxic ,but then evolved into a negative place. Again, resorting back to the chapter on boundaries, we hold the responsibility to ensure we are not tolerating behaviors that are inappropriate and toxic. Not only do we have to protect ourselves, but we must hold a protective space for our children and our partners. So, if you have a toxic relationship with a family member, it is up to you to decide on how to mitigate that. If you feel comfortable having a conversation with that individual, then that might be the route to go. However, typically in toxic situations, more often than not, the toxic family member is not going to receive your message in a positive way nor will they respond in the way you asked for them to. Toxicity is the result of their own trauma and their own unresolved issues. Remember, their response to your choices is not part of your journey. Only you can make the determination on how to move forward. Some people may feel ok with consistently reminding the toxic individual of the rules regarding how to engage with you. Toxic people tend to be triggered by the enforcement of boundaries. The trauma response and fear based emotional thinking is engaged before rational thought can be expected. This is OK. Remember, you are gravitating towards a new role and a new space for your life. Joy has no time for toxicity. The only issues we can positively affect are our own. We cannot change the way other people treat us. We can only choose to decide on what we will and will not tolerate. We can release these relationships without anger or hatred. We release these relationships in a positive frame of mind and wish these individuals well. Expressing gratitude for having known them and having had the opportunity to engage with them will only fast-track your growth and wellness. Our wellness depends upon our willingness to enforce these boundaries. We get to decide who has access to us. If a person doesn't treat you with love and kindness, then do you continue to allow them to participate in your life? It's ok to be fed-up. In fact, it is healthy to get to a place where you are willing and able to say, "no more."

Changing how we live can manifest in many ways. We can decide that we want to eat healthier, exercise more, and stop abusing drugs and alcohol. We can also decide to give up on trying to improve our lives for the better. We can be influenced by the effects of those individuals in our lives, as well as the influence of mental struggles, such as depression and anxiety. For anyone who has ever struggled with mental illness, they understand all too well the calling of drugs and alcohol to make the pain go away, if only for a little while. Sometimes food is used as a coping mechanism to just "get through the day". Nicotine is another form of coping that people use. Everyone who uses something to pacify whatever adverse condition in their life knows the long-term effects are considered unhealthy, so why do they keep doing it? It's easy to understand the benefits of adopting a healthy lifestyle. It's harder to implement. Afterall, if a smoker were to give up cigarettes, how would they mitigate stress and anxiety? Additionally, would the smoker be able to conduct a thorough personal inventory to identify the causes of stress and anxiety? It's not likely, which is why it seems easier to maintain the status quo, no matter how unhealthy it is in the long run.

Fear of failing when someone decides to quit smoking or lose weight is another barrier to change. Why bother if it won't lead to success? Why is the overweight person overweight to begin with? Is it a sedentary lifestyle? Is it unhealthy food choices? Is it both, perhaps? Maybe the overweight person believes that because everyone in their family is overweight, it's more of a genetic issue, therefore reinforcing the expectation of failing to lose the weight and keep it off. There are endless reasons people avoid change. It's important to be able to identify the worthiness of the individual who is attempting to make a change. If a smoker wants to quit smoking, then it's key for that person to stop smoking because they believe that they deserve to be healthy and they deserve to be able to lead a smoke free lifestyle. A smoker needs to believe that they deserve to better understand the reasons they started smoking to begin with. Anyone attempting to make changes should identify their own value first and understand that they deserve to try to change. They deserve the opportunity to fail and try again without judgment and blame.

Amazing things happen when we simply believe that we are worthy of amazing things.

You deserve amazing things because you are amazing.

CHAPTER FIVE

CLARITY

When you think about your life and where you've been and how far you've come, do you ever find yourself feeling regretful, or even ashamed, of some of the decisions that you've made? The truth is, that we have all grown from our experiences and had it not been for our experiences, we simply would not be where we are today. We grow and we learn. It is not fair to use a present-day lens built with life wisdom to view decisions made in the past, when we did not possess that wisdom. Can you imagine being a 45-year-old woman thinking back on a time when she was 9 years old and drove her bicycle off the side of a rocky ledge and ended up breaking her bike and her wrist? Imagine that 45-year-old woman imparting the life wisdom gained over the years to judge the 9-year-old self. It happens all the time, but it's not something that we consciously take care and consideration to avoid. The 9-year-old child does not deserve to be judged harshly through a 45-year-old viewpoint. The 9-year-old only knows what they have accumulated in 9 years of life. While unfortunate, the 9-year-old made a choice and learned from it. It's that simple.

We tend to be critical and unfair to ourselves in ways we would never imagine treating anyone else. Culture teaches us that we owe more to others than to ourselves, mostly out of the demonstration of this behavior by care-givers during childhood and adolescence. We see others acting this way, and as a result, adopt the same ideals; right or wrong. It is a part of who we are and nothing more. While we may feel a little silly thinking back on the decisions we've made, whether those decisions were a type of vehicle we purchased or even someone we dated much longer than we should have, we end up needing these experiences in order to grow and be the people we are today. I use many of my own life experiences in this book, and as such, I'm certain that many of them will color the dialogue that I choose to share with you. Authenticity is another chapter which details how critical it is to become the best version of yourself. In order to be authentic, we must accept our past and our past deci-sions as a part of who we are today. Judgment and blame are not only not necessary in this process, they are irrele-vant to healing and growth. We must fully embrace who we used to be in order to fully understand what we were and to provide the clarity we need in becoming the best version of ourselves today. All human beings are inher-ently fallible. Making mistakes is part of the fabric of the human experience.

Mistakes are not indicative of a person's character. They are merely a part of life.

Sometimes I find myself disclosing my own personal experiences with my clients not only as a measure of commonality and connection to build the rapport that is necessary, but to also validate their feelings of discomfort in relating to past choices. While this isn't an approach that all therapists subscribe to it is something that I feel is crucial in building the kind of support I feel is necessary to help others. The biggest fear we all have in this life is lack of connection to others. When a person seeks mental health help, they are already in a vulnerable space. It is my belief that my role in this is to provide as much safety as possible for my client to heal. I can also volunteer that I derive both personal and professional satisfaction out of being able to provide the support necessary to create the fertile foundation for healing for my clients. In my own journey to wellness and clarity, I can detail many instances where I experienced personal growth. For example, I can recall with specific detail the reasons I had in joining the military. I can tell you without hesitation, it had nothing to do with a sense of patriotic duty to my nation (see chapter on cultural influences), but instead my growing desire to isolate a path for my own future. However, my journey to be a part of the military did not begin with my enlistment into the Air Force. My original plan was to marry a military man and have him take me out of Alabama as far away as possible. The schemas that I had at the time were influenced by my family, my social circles and southern cultural rules. As a woman, it was frowned upon for me to serve in the military. No one actually said it to my face (besides an ignorant, elderly great aunt who expressed disdain for my life choices, I digress). Many folks who had been employed as laborers in the factory where I worked were confused as to why I would "give up" my life of operating an automated commercial sewing machine by joining the military, when I could easily just get married and start a family. The irony in all of this was it was my original plan to do just that, prior to deciding to enlist in the Air Force. However, my ex-boyfriend had other plans and extricated himself from my life. So, plan A wasn't going to work to get me out of Alabama.

On to plan B.

As my luck would have it, I had been out of high school for three years and did not have any long-term plans for my future, financial or otherwise. My boyfriend of one year broke up with me, causing me to lose my plans for my future. When I say lost, I mean he chose to end the relationship. Looking back on my situation in third person, I see a young woman setting her claws into an unsuspecting young man who was trying to figure out his own life. I see a young woman so insecure and broken experiencing wholeness for the first time in her life. She felt pretty and accepted. She felt loved. As a result, she abandoned any sense of opinion and as a measure of maintaining this relationship she subscribed to any opinion or desire of her boyfriend. Looking back, I can remember how the relationship was the first time I'd ever felt like I was going to be "ok". It wasn't even on my conscious mind to consider having an opinion on anything. The only thing I ever wanted from my boyfriend was for him to marry me and take me out of Alabama, far away from my life, my fears, and my deeply rooted pain. Bear in mind, I can now reflect on who I was and the commonality in my life choices, but at the time to me in my young unwise and scattered and traumatized mindset, was utterly clueless to the interconnectedness of all these events. I can clearly see now, how my behavior placed a tremendous amount of pressure on my boyfriend who was simply not ready to get married. He broke up with me over the phone and the depth of pain I felt resonates with me to this day, though I now understand it. I now have empathy for my then boyfriend, as a woman who has evolved and experienced tremendous personal growth and healing. Back then, however, I could only feel fury. I did everything I was supposed to do as a girlfriend in the relationship and, yet, it still wasn't enough. When he broke up with me, it triggered my deeply rooted belief that I was not lovable. That metastasized into a level of anger I was not prepared for. What I didn't understand at the time was that my hostility towards my now ex-boyfriend played a pivotal role in my newfound strength and confidence in joining the military. In the tenure of our relationship and with my need to maintain his happiness and my own sense of safety, I ignored his personal judgments and culturally insensitive comments about women and minorities. I did not agree with him, but I loved him and wanted nothing more than to make him happy. So, I ignored his racist and sexist commentary. Off and on during the relationship, he had made several statements regarding his personal devaluation of women in military service. Because he provided a sense of safety, both financially as well as a dysfunctional sense of emotional safety, I acquiesced to his opinions regarding women in service. Afterall, if he had agreed to marry me then he would essentially have been "saving me" and I should be grateful to him for that. When he terminated the relationship, I contemplated his previous comments about women in the

Military. "Women are not fit to wear a military beret." "Women with tattoos are trashy." "Women are not fit to be soldiers." All these sentiments replayed over and over in my head to the point where it became very clear to me that as a measure to prove him wrong, I simply had no choice but to join the service.

Blinding white rage.

I called a recruiter and signed up for the Air Force.

I asked a friend of mine to ride with me to the tattoo parlor.

Keep in mind, this is 20 something years ago and I had been raised to believe I was not that smart and was not of the ilk or worthiness of attending college. In fairness, my grades in high school were not what you would consider "ideal" for matriculating. My confidence in attending higher education would come many years later. All of this to say, my plan was to marry someone who would take care of me. Much of my gratitude today is wrapped up in the fact that this individual elected to set me free at the time that he did. So, in conjunction with my beliefs about my lower intelligence, my female gender, and my overall low-quality as a human being in general, combined with my rage were used as fuel to push me through my military training. To add humor, I remember clearly that I had elected to enlist as a security police officer in the US Air Force so that I would be armed with a firearm in a law-enforcement capacity. I chose to become a security police officer with the applicable headwear (beret) for the sole reason of proving a point.

Do you have a story like this? Can you think back to younger days and remember how you used to feel about yourself and your beliefs about who you were? Do you ever feel like you carry regret about an event in your life that you wish you would have handled differently? What is that event? Does it involve anyone else? If so, was the other person involved offended, insulted, or harmed by your choices in any way? *Digging deeper* Did you ever take ownership of your cause of injury/harm to this person? Why or why not? Remember, and I will continue to remind you the reader, that this is not a "fault finding mission". It's about finding truth and isolating where our demons lie and learning how to reframe and let go of issues like this that weigh us down.

I have a clear understanding of who I was back then. I also understand how that affected the choices that I made. I'm grateful for my time in the military. Albeit unintentional, a side effect of my military service was my ability to remove myself from the conditions of my childhood environment and take advantage of this newfound opportunity of redefining who and what I was. Everyone back home had an opinion of me, or so I assumed. I was not smart and did not come from a family with a good reputation. Everyone back home knew this. My military colleagues did not know this about me and, if they did, it's highly likely that they would not have cared. Being in basic training offered an opportunity for personal growth unlike any other conditions I'd ever experienced. My training instructors were there to ensure I met my training requirements and nothing more. My training instructors did not care if I succeeded or failed. My success was entirely up to me. I was afforded the same opportunities as the other airmen in my flight and when I graduated basic training, it meant more to me than graduating high school. In fact, it still does to this day. It was the first time in my life when I started to feel as though I could accomplish my goals. If I could successfully complete basic training, then what else was I capable of accomplishing?

Finding clarity about our life's choices and how those choices have shaped who we are today can be a heart wrenching and often bittersweet evolution, but it is critical to continue pushing forward and doing the necessary groundwork to move out of shame and pain and into growth, renewal, and healing. This is the only way to live life with joy and love.

I know without question that had I not had these experiences, I simply would not be where I am today. Therefore, I am deeply grateful for all the hurt and pain that drove me into a situation where I was able to reevaluate my self-worth and my own intellect. It's difficult for me to imagine a scenario without military service that would have challenged me to push past my own fear-based opinions about myself and learn to cultivate confidence. It's equally difficult for me to imagine a different scenario that would have propelled me to willingly choose to join the military without having a broken heart fueled by blinding rage. I had been tolerant in my own insecurities and low sense of worth prior to this relationship. It is impossible for me to imagine willfully enlisting in the military with the submissive frame of mind I was in before I met my then boyfriend. That relationship and subsequent break-up created an emotional storm in me that, without these experiences, I don't think that I would be living a life that is nearly as fulfilling as the one I have today. While painful at the time, I can intertwine these individual experiences into a rich and full history that has propelled me to here. I am deeply grateful.

What is your narrative? What choices have you made in your past that have brought you to where you are today? More to the point, are you where you want to be? What do you need to do in order to get where you want to be? Are you around the right people? Are you being encouraged? If not, why? I share these stories with you because I understand the pressures of being around stronger personalities and how they can affect your own reality in ways that ,on the surface, do not seem to make sense. The truth is, you can become a better version of yourself. You can make choices to extricate yourself from situations, people, relationships, and jobs etc., that are holding you back from being who you really need to be. It's not easy to climb a mountain, but it can be done. When you find clarity in the choices that you have made, and you are honest with yourself about why you've made these choices, you are able to start reclaiming your own gifts that you have unknowingly surrendered. Perhaps you gave your gifts to other people with the expectation that they will make your life easier or better? I know I did that in a handful of subsequent relationships after I left military service. It's not a perfect process because growth never is.

Finding clarity in your life can be difficult simply because we are afraid of what we will see. I want you to know it's ok. You're ok. You're worthy and a part of a greater consciousness. You are no better and no worse than your fellow man because we are all connected and worthy. You deserve the opportunity to conduct a review of your previous choices as a measure of better understanding who you are now versus who you used to be. You may see some things about yourself that make you feel ashamed.

Again, remember this is about learning and growing. It is not about judgment and blame. Remember to think back on why you acted the way you did and give yourself the grace and fairness, even if you don't think that you deserve it. Once you start thinking this way, you will learn to be kinder to yourself and, as a result, your actions will follow in love-based thinking.

Have you ever carried something so heavy and for so long you relished the thought of putting it down? Did you ever think you "wouldn't make it" because it's so heavy? Can you remember the relief of setting it down? How many times have you attempted to bring groceries into the house in one trip? It feels good to put them down, doesn't it? Emotional clarity works in much the same way. We carry lifelong burdens, unnecessarily, for so long, we don't even realize we're so overwhelmed and burdened. You deserve understanding and clarity in finding out what those burdens are, and you deserve the opportunity to be accountable and to take ownership of your mistakes that caused harm to others. You deserve to understand your reasons for your choices, and you deserve to forgive yourself.

What are you carrying around? If you've harmed someone in your past and you want to "fix it," what would that look like? Sometimes, we are not able to reach out to those we've harmed, as a measure of righting the wrongs. Furthermore, we can sometimes create more harm by bringing up the past. Perhaps you feel you're being punished by carrying around the shame of an event you engaged in that manifested in a mistake of some kind. Perhaps the person that you harmed is nowhere to be found. Perhaps that person has passed on. When you explore the reasons for the decisions you made that harmed others, only then will you find the clarity necessary in order to forgive yourself, even if others don't.

CHAPTER SIX

ACCOUNTABILITY

Let's talk about what it means to be accountable. Why do so many people have a hard time accepting blame when they make an error? Do you have a hard time accepting blame? I know I do. In fact, while conducting research and writing this book, I was pushing this chapter off into a far corner of my mind simply because my subconscious did not want to deal with my need to be accountable. Nobody wants to be at fault. It sucks to be wrong. It makes us feel small and less worthy as human beings. When we admit fault, we somehow feel as though we are opening to the judgments of others and in truth we are, technically. Fortunately, for us, when we screw up, the judgment of others is irrelevant to our own healing. It does not matter that other people revel in our errors. This is a fear-based behavior on their part and is something for them to work through. It is a projection of their own need to protect their veneer. What is important to our own healing is that we are able to identify the thinking errors in other people. While it still happens, it is entirely egocentric (natural self-ishness based in human development theory attributed to the behaviors of small children) to allow the judgments of other people to negatively affect us. Granted, this is easier said than done, but we must start somewhere and knowing what this behavior is when it manifests in our world will provide us with the ability to distinguish our healing and growth from other people's negative projections towards us. Wouldn't it be ideal to not actually care when other people seek to injure us with their negative judgment? It's nice to think that when other people find flaws in us that it is merely a projection of their own need to protect themselves and nothing more, even if the assertion is accurate.

Fear of being judged is a roadblock to accountability. Acceptance of deserved judgment is part of the accountability process.

Imagine you are in a hurry to get to work. As you pull into the parking lot you accidentally ding the passenger side door of your co-worker's brand-new minivan. This co-worker already doesn't like you, so this will not be an easy fix. You go inside your building and you locate your co-worker and you tell her you've just dinged her minivan. She leaps from her chair and rushes outside to survey the damage. You're already feeling she's being overly dramatic and are feeling regret for even pointing out the damage to her. You could have just parked somewhere else and not said anything. No big deal, right? No one else would know. Only you. You would know. You would know, and at a subconscious level, you wouldn't appreciate it if someone dinged your car and then didn't tell you about it. She sees the damage and snarls at you, "I suppose you've got insurance to fix this?" "My deductible is more than what it would cost to fix the damage. If you will take it to your body shop have them send me the bill, I could pick you up and drop you off while your car is in the shop." "Well that's not going to help me pick my kids up from day care. You don't have room in your car to do that." "I tell you what, go to the body shop ask them if they have a loaner vehicle. If they don't, let me know and I'll rent you a vehicle while yours is in the shop." "Whatever."

Have you ever tried to fix a situation with someone and, no matter what you did or how hard you tried, it never seems to be enough? Sometimes, people don't want others to get out of their obligation to them. Sometimes people fester in their own drama as a need to magnify their own sense of victimhood. It happens. You still need to be accountable, regardless of your co-worker's response to you. You dinged the car and therefore you are responsible. You may not always get a positive outcome, but you must do the right thing for your own well-being.

When we accept accountability for our errors, we can't help but grow and heal from the experience, despite a negative response from others.

A crucial aspect of accountability is understanding how it creates the foundation for learning to recognize when we need to change our ways. When we learn to be accountable, we are sensitive to our behaviors in the future and how to prevent the manifestation of situations that would need to be mitigated. The scenario above would most likely encourage you to slow down when driving through the parking lot at work, don't you think?

We know that we are accountable, so we are careful about what we do in ways that hold space for us to be careful and compassionate, not just to others, but to ourselves as well. Often, accountability involves other people. When we hurt someone that we are supposed to love, it can be emotionally excruciating to conclude that we caused harm to that person. The shame we feel in these situations is a weight that many of us can't imagine. Many times, we construct a delusion as a measure to distract us from being accountable and accepting responsibility for our behavior to avoid this feeling of shame. But, as we do this, we only magnify the error.

Imagine you're at your spouse's holiday office party and you drink too much. Your spouse's boss comes up to chat about the upcoming new year and to ask you about your new house you're building. However, you decide to make fun of his tie and then ask him if his wife ever found out that he was sleeping with his secretary. Your spouse is horrified. "What?? I was just kidding!" You were, after all, quite inebriated and thought that it would be funny to insinuate that your spouse's boss was having an affair with his secretary. Your spouse turns to you and says "That's it. We are going home." The next day, you remember your comment and apologize to your spouse profusely. She/he is mortified that you would do some-thing like that. You offer to call the boss and apologize but she/he won't hear of it. You feel ashamed and defensive. She/he doesn't need to be THAT harsh does she/he? "It was a party. Everyone was drinking" You try to minimize and devalue the damage your words caused. You can see that your spouse is crying and won't speak to you. Your shame is overwhelming.

How would you handle a situation like this? What is it about this situation that makes you accountable for how your spouse feels? How do you think your spouse feels when you invalidate her/his emotional response to your actions?

Do you see how our own emotional response to our shame spirals downward when we are faced with the inevitability of accepting responsibility for our actions? Just because you love someone doesn't mean that you won't occasionally hurt them. It's an unfortunate side effect of being a human being. However, the bigger insult comes from the denial of accountability in these situations. Not only do you deny the responsibility of your actions, but you further injure the one you initially hurt through invalidating their emotional response. "You're over-reacting."

"It wasn't that big of a deal." "Your boss was probably drunk too. I doubt he will remember."

Being accountable means taking ownership of, both intended and unintended, behaviors. Just because a person hits your car on accident doesn't mean they are less responsible for the error. The same goes with our behaviors and how they affect those around us. You may not have intended to cause harm, but you are responsible just the same and, thus, deserve the opportunity to right the error.

So, we all know that we need to accept responsibility but that doesn't mean that we actually do it. So, instead of focusing this chapter on the nuances of accountability, let's talk about the benefits of accountability and how it affects our relationships with other people. By doing this, we learn how to understand how profound these influences are and, as a result, we can be easier on ourselves and not be so hard and judgmental when we look inward.

Recently, I have had the ability to identify my thinking errors, as well as how those errors in behaviors have affected my own relationships. Of course, I believe I am a good person, however my behavior through my own triggers and emotional responses have, at times, been my reasoning for poor and or otherwise harmful behaviors.

My experiences as a child, while adverse at times, cultivated in me a belief about myself that was neither conducive towards a responsible attitude nor was it functional in a healthy relationship. Had I not embarked on this journey of growth, I would probably still be engaging in a lot of those behaviors today. However, I am here to say that I have made many mistakes that have hurt other people and I have treated people that I love with bitterness and resentment and hostility undeservedly. I hold myself accountable because I deserve to be a better person and I deserve good people in my life and those good people deserve the best possible version of me. I am the only person who can do this work, just as you, the reader, are the only person who can do the work in your life, too. No matter what adverse conditions you grew up in and no matter who harmed you or who convinced you that you are a "bad person" (you're not by the way) and unworthy, know this: anything that you attribute to yourself as adverse is an excuse to avoid accountability in your life and, if you avoid accountability, you avoid happiness and you avoid joy and you avoid peace in your spirit and heart. You deserve all these things simply because you're here.

Not only do you HAVE purpose, but you ARE purpose.

All living creatures are responsible for coming to this existence and coming to this place we call life in the best version of themselves. When you mess up, you must give yourself grace and understand why you did what you did and clean up the mess with kindness and love for yourself. If you walk into the kitchen and you drop a glass of water onto the floor, you can stand there and tell everyone, "Hey, look at me. I'm a piece of crap because I broke the glass!" All while walking away from the mess and feeling broken and worthless because you broke the glass. Or you can look at the glass and look at everyone around you and tell them, "I broke this glass. I didn't mean to. It was an accident. Can someone show me where the broom and dustpan and the towels are so that I can clean this up?" Simply put, the glass is not going to clean itself up. Beating yourself up and walking away from a mess that you created is not helpful. You're not a bad person if you broke the glass but if you consistently come into the kitchen and break glasses and then admit that you broke the glass, all while being self-deprecating, that's not helpful either, is it?

Why did you break the glass? Were you being careless? Did you see the glass on the side of the counter as you walked into the kitchen and deliberately knock it off the countertop? If you meant to knock the glass over, then accepting accountability for something you did on purpose has a different meaning. You must now understand why you broke the glass on purpose. Were you trying to get attention? Did you want the people in the kitchen to feel bad for you? The questions we can answer for ourselves are endless regarding identifying the reasons we make mistakes or engage in various types of dysfunctional behaviors. True clarity comes from not only acknowledging the error but making amends and that means cleaning the mess.

What messes have you made? What do you need to clean up?

CHAPTER SEVEN

FEAR

Fear is not a bad thing, per se. If you are fearful, then you tend to avoid dangerous situations, in theory. Fear keeps you away from the edge, from leaning too close to the void of the unknown. Fear keeps you encapsulated, like a burrito, wrapped up in the façade of safety. Perhaps, it's not necessarily a façade, but it is the reality of safety. So, while you are safe, nestled within a particular circumstance, an OK job, a lukewarm yet unsatisfying and unfulfilling relationship, consistently engaging with individuals in your family and friendship and professional circles with whom you have no passion and no legitimate and genuine connection to, out of fear, then you are missing out on your full and whole potential.

Fear of failure.

What does the voice in the back of your head say to you in the early light of day, or perhaps during a quick lull in your workday, about what you really want out of life?

Does fear jump in and mitigate and squash those thoughts and feelings?

Late at night, when the voices in your head hold space and compete for your attention, which ones come out on top?

Are there voices that tell you to stay where you are and to not take chances?

Perhaps, occasionally, you hear a different voice. This is the voice that sometimes challenges you to rise above mediocrity. This voice gains your attention, if only for a moment, and causes your heart to beat a little faster because of it. For a fleeting moment, you get a little excited about what might be and what could be. Perhaps you feel the wholeness of your potential and you are awash in inspiration and gratitude for what you have and what you can have. What happens in these moments? Does fear run in and shut this moment down?

Maybe you used to have them, but you don't anymore.

Why is this?

What's the purpose in reading this book at all?

What are you looking for?

Rational versus irrational fears

Taking inventory of your environment, whatever that may look like, is always going to be something different for everyone. It is a logical assessment to be mindful of what choices you should make regarding a healthy and fruitful outcome of your day. For instance, if you live or work in a neighborhood with questionable security issues, then, obviously, you would take measures to ensure you protect yourself and your family. This is common logic and is something that is done to stay safe. This is logical fear. If you know you're at risk, then you take necessary measures to mitigate that risk. The same could be said for visiting a new area, which might not necessarily be unsafe, but if you're unfamiliar with certain territory, then you would want to take precautions to protect yourself. The same can go for embarking upon any new venture within your life whether that be a personal relationship, a new job, purchasing a new home, or any other major life event where the outcome is largely unpredictable. But you wouldn't, in theory, engage in any of these activities without conducting a reasonable risk assessment, right? This is where we get into the weeds when discussing fear and choices. Often, we make choices because the fear we have in our current circumstances causes us to move into directions we have not fully investigated. This is when fear repeats a cycle in our lives. When we don't take the time to be present and mindful and conscious in the decisions we make in our lives, fear will always dominate.

Shelly (not her real name) came home from a work trip to an empty house and a note. Her husband had left. She knew something was up when he quit replying to her text messages two days ago. If she were being truly honest with herself, she knew long before that there were problems in their marriage. Shelly met Brian three years earlier on a different work trip when they were both staying at the same hotel. Brian was there on a work conference from a town near where Shelly lived. They had a conversation at the bar that serviced both of their respective work functions and decided to have dinner the next evening. At the time, Shelly had just broken up with her previous boyfriend when she'd discovered he'd been unfaithful. In Shelly's mind, meeting Brian was the best thing that could have happened to her. They had dinner and agreed to meet again for another date at mini golf when they both traveled back to their home state. Because they met at a bar five states away and because they lived so close to each other, Shelly attributed this as fate. She and Brian dated for six months before they moved in together. Six months later, they were married in an impromptu ceremony in Las Vegas. Shelly said that she'd always wanted a beautiful wedding, but she let that dream go when Brian stated that he would be willing to marry her if they didn't have a big wedding. Shelly willingly agreed. "It was just a waste of money to feed people that we never see anyway," she justified. So, they drove to Las Vegas and were married in a quickie ceremony followed by a steak dinner and a burlesque review show. Again, not exactly how Shelly had envisioned her honeymoon, but she loved Brian and he was sweet. Over the next two years Shelly received two promotions at work and, as a result, was required to travel more frequently on business. Brian appeared to understand this, and he enjoyed the extra money that Shelly was bringing home. On one occasion, she returned a day early to find a brand-new set of golf clubs in the living room. She knew Brian did not have the money to purchase the clubs, so she checked their joint savings account. "$1500 for golf clubs?" It was unbelievable. They had never had a fight and Shelly was angry, but at the same time, fearful. She was afraid if she argued with Brian about the golf clubs, that he would leave. After all, her parents used to argue all the time and it made her physically ill to hear people argue. She'd always swore she'd never be in a relationship where there was fighting. So, Shelly moved the clubs into the spare bedroom out of the way of foot traffic and never mentioned them or the missing money to Brian. Flash forward to now, Shelly read the note from Brian and grew increasingly afraid. Maybe if she could talk to him, she could convince him to try again. Maybe they could go to therapy? She looked around the house. All her things were still there and, even many of Brian's things, he'd also left. She looked for the golf clubs, but those were gone. "Wow. That's all I'm worth to him. $1500 worth of sporting equipment." Shelly began to cry. She didn't know what to do. She texted her girlfriend to come over. They sat down, drank a bottle of wine, and her friend proceeded to unload all her opinions about Brian. This made Shelly feel worse and she went to the bathroom to throw up. "What am I going to do?" she sobbed. "I can't be alone." Shelly's friend held her until she fell asleep on the sofa, then let herself out and closed the door.

What do you think Shelly is afraid of?

How does fear manifest in Shelly's decision-making ability to do what is in her long-term best interest?

Do you relate to Shelly or do you know someone who reminds you of Shelly?

We become prisoners to our own circumstances because of our feelings of powerlessness when it comes to fear. What is fear anyway? What is the purpose of being fearful? From an evolutionary perspective, one could argue that fear has the purpose of preventing injury or death to oneself by creating a sense of hyper awareness to one's own circumstances. So, understanding the purpose behind being afraid to begin with can help with navigating the confusion that is caused when we are not present and conscious in making decisions. This is why presence of mind, mindfulness, being grounded, and taking the time to be conscious about our choices of what we think and feel, is critical to our own pursuit of success and joy and actualization.

Without this, fear will always dominate the landscape of our thoughts and feelings.

When we are mindful and our thoughts are clear, we are less likely to make decisions from a fear-based mindset.

Take a moment and consider what you are fearful of. When you do this, be mindful of the circumstances of your life which you have no control over. Are you fearful of losing a loved one? Do you have a loved one that is suffering from an illness and you are fearful of what the future holds for them? Are you fearful of flying? Perhaps you have left an unfulfilling relationship and due to that experience, you are fearful of ever considering connecting with another person again. Assessing one's own fear is the first step to assessing future choices. While there is very little that you can do to change the outcome of a dire medical diagnosis of a love one, you can most certainly change the way you engage with that person in the present. If you are fearful of a future relationship's potential, then perhaps you take time to fully conduct the forensics of your past relationships and define key points where you were not fully aware or conscious in your decision making. Perhaps you gave an unworthy person time they did not deserve. Perhaps you made choices in your previous relationship that eroded your sense of self. Fear can be tricky because, without the investigation of our past thinking errors, we are most likely to make those same choices again. This knowledge in and of itself is fertile ground for fear in our minds and hearts to grow.

Knowledge and understanding are the equivalent of a fire extinguisher to a fire when battling fear. Unhealthy fear-based thinking is rooted in ignorance. It is not an assessment of character to be fearful but is only a lack of information.

If you want to achieve a goal but you're afraid to try, why is that?

Are you fearful of failing?

What happens if you try and you fail?

What does it mean to fail?

Do you have a belief about yourself that you are unwilling, unable, lazy, undeserving etc. to achieve your goals?

Are there people in your life who will criticize your attempt to succeed?

Are there individuals you know who will critique your attempts to achieve something better? Are you surrounded by individuals who are toxic and who want you to remain in the status quo with them?

Would they see you as betraying them when you attempt to achieve your goals?

Are you self-deprecating?

Do you look in the mirror and see failure?

External validation is a wonderful and beautiful and deeply gratifying experience. It feels good when other people cheer us on. However, we cannot exist and succeed and thrive on external validation alone. Value and validation and worthiness come from the unquestionable understanding that we are all interconnected within the universe. We are all equal and therefore, by default, we are all worthy of succeeding and achieving our goals, whatever those goals may look like. When we fully grasp this concept, our entire cognitive structure and beliefs about ourselves in the world that we live in evolves in such a magnificent way that we are able to look back at any of the naysayers in our environment with empathy and compassion and understand their need to criticize and discourage us is only a byproduct of their own fear, not yours.

Do you look in the mirror and know that you have caused harm to others and, because of this, you do not deserve to achieve your goals? (See the chapter on accountability and how these two dynamics of fear and accountability interplay with each other.)

Are you fearful of the amount of investment and energy you would have to expend in order to achieve your goal?

Do you feel maybe you're not up to the task?

Why do you have the goal to begin with?

What would change in your life if you achieved your goals?

The changes you seek to make are your own. Only you can decide whether they are justified, logical, purposeful and worthy. Only you can determine the roadblocks in your mind and heart in achieving your goals.

Even when we conduct a thorough assessment of what our goals look like and how they will affect our current situation and relationships, there will always be distractions and uncomfortable revelations about the true motivations of those individuals in our lives. Of course, we must consider our choices and how they affect our loved ones and our professional and social relationships but, again, you were the only one that can assess the worthiness of your choices and your goals.

So, what are you afraid of? What do you want to change? What do you want to start or stop doing in your life? What do you want to feel when you look in the mirror?

Remember this: You are your biggest hero and you also are your biggest obstacle in achieving success.

CHAPTER EIGHT

WORTHINESS

Can you think back to your very early childhood and recall your well-being and sense of self? Understandably, most people can't or, for whatever reason, are unwilling to do this. But the ultimate question is to determine at what point in your life did you make a self-assessment of what your value and worth really is as a person. What influences in your life cause you to feel how you feel about yourself today? If you are to really be genuine and authentic with yourself, without reservation, what would you say about yourself? What defining adjectives would you purposefully use to describe the person that you are? One common factor that runs rampant within clinical circles is a sense of low self-worth. If you are one of these individuals who feels a very low sense of self-worth, I'm here to tell you that is complete and total garbage. Now, we are talking about behaviors. Your behavior is something that you are responsible for. If you have done things that harm yourself and or other people, then I will refer you back to the accountability chapter. Even so, if you are guilty of perpetuating harmful behaviors, whether to yourself or other people, I am telling you, that if you feel badly about yourself, then that is a thinking error. If you place your hand on your chest and ever so carefully pay attention to the rise and fall of your breathing in the regular thump-thump sensation, then you, my friend, have value and purpose.

Oh yes, there's always going to be one or two people who will dismiss this for a variety of reasons. As a young social worker, I facilitated a support group for adult women survivors of childhood sexual trauma. Now, before you bristle at the potential of being triggered by a graphic detail, I am here to reassure you that I do not intend to go into the graphic details. However, there may be some troubling dynamics, so please read on in a mindful state and take a break if necessary. These women were incredible in their resiliency and their humor and intellect and their passion. One of these ladies detailed her history of abuse within their family church. Apparently, from a very young age, her parents believed that in order to become closer to God, that they should allow their children to be used as an offering to the elders of the church for sexual gratification. Her interpretation of her own sexuality manifested as being the marker of her value as an individual. One of the issues she was working through in therapy was to be able to isolate a sense of wellness within herself that was not attached to her body. She did not hate herself. She simply did not feel entitled to a sense of well-being beyond being a sexual object for the gratification of others.

Years later, I had another client who disclosed to me she had been conceived in rape and was put up for adoption as an infant. Her adoptive parents were manipulative and emotionally abusive towards her through their indication that if she did not completely adhere to the doctrine and live her life with fervent adherence to the gospel within their church, she would most definitely spend all eternity in the fires of hell due to the nature of her conception.

Her distress brought her to attempting suicide on several occasions.

I want you to know something. It is entirely up to you whether you believe what I have to say in this book. I can only share my interpretations of the world as I see it, both as an individual and as a therapist. What I do know, is that I have seen more trauma caused by organized religious zealots than I have witnessed my clients benefiting in a positive way. I say organized religious zealots because there are many faith and spiritual paths that work towards the betterment of the individual, as opposed to utilizing doctrine as a measure of control over large swaths of people. In other words, church and a spiritual community is healthy and helpful if it is used to educate, teach, and grow a community towards a healthy and encouraging spiritual path. Groups of people who use organized faith and texts to marginalize and control and indoctrinate various groups of people are not healthy and lead to cognitive dissonance and a host of mental issues.

It is up to you to choose what you want to believe about yourself and about your self-worth. That is the beginning of self-healing and recovery. There is nothing I can do or say or write down in this chapter or any other chapter or any other book, that can convince you otherwise until you want to believe that you deserve to see yourself in a positive light. You don't necessarily have to believe what I say, you just must want to change how you live your life. You may find other ways that lead you into your own path of healing and, ultimately, that is my goal of this writing.

Do you want to believe that you're worth experiencing joy and love and happiness? Do you want to believe that you deserve to live with purpose? Do you want to believe that you deserve to go through your life without regret and without the infliction of injury from those around you who profess to care and love you? Are you surrounded by people who seek to control you and put you down?

The truth lives within you. You just must believe it. I can tell you that the people that raised you or influenced you in your life perhaps at church or at school, who said hurtful things about you were wrong. They are wrong and they were wrong to tell you that you are worth less than someone who was born to a couple who was married versus being conceived in rape. It isn't right to believe that your body serves as a conduit for the sexual gratification for people who profess to be the purveyors of the gospel. It is a horrible concept to imagine the depths of despair and trauma that so many people experience throughout their lives as a direct result of the consequence of their conception.

No one deserves to deal with that kind of baggage. It is a false narrative. It is untrue.

While horrific, the abuse that children endure and feel compelled to carry throughout their lives, is not indicative of their value as human beings.

No one can ever do anything to you that erodes your value as a human being. If you're reading this, you are worthy.

The consequences and circumstances of your conception are irrelevant to your value as a human being.

Your value as a human being is equal to every other human being ever conceived on this planet in all of history and in all the future.

There is no pedigree, religion, ethnicity, gender, sexuality, able or disabled, marker that increases or decreases your value as a human being. Read that again.

You, and only you, get to determine your worth. If you think that you are worthless, but you want to think that you are worthy, then all you must do is to believe that you deserve to believe it.

You do not need to worry about so-called friends, family, acquaintances, coworkers, people on the street, etc. expressing their judgmental attitude towards who you are and what your value is. Other people's opinions do not matter when it comes to identifying your own value in your own worthiness. Remember, other people's opinions of you are none of your business.

I realize that the reality is there is racism and sexism and classism that is rampant all over the world. What I am discussing, however, is the ability to identify oneself with worth despite all the external garbage. It is garbage because it is untrue. It's a cultural influence that dictates these thinking errors. It's up to you to challenge them.

You get to decide your worth. You get to decide what kind of person you want to be. A person who believes they are worthy of good things, will do good things. Your character is directly related to the positive influence you bring into the world. Change is hard. Change is also worth it. If you don't think that you're a good person then what do you need to do to change that?

See the chapter on accountability for more details and fun facts

CHAPTER NINE

TOXIC BEHAVIORS

I touch on some of the aspect of toxic influences in our lives in the Fear chapter. Refer to Fear for more details.

So, let's get down to it. Let's be honest here. Are there individuals in your life that are holding you in a space of stagnation? In other words, if you were to contemplate making some significant changes and how you manifest and move through this life, would you be judged negatively for making these changes? Do you feel unfairly categorized and labeled by certain individuals in your life?

Are these the same people that were in the front row of the audience during our fear to love exercise in chapter one?

Have these people imbedded themselves in your life in ways that make you feel obligated to them?

Are you fearful of these people and their responses to your choices?

Do you often tolerate bad behavior in people?

Keep in mind, when we allow other people to behave negatively and to express toxic behavior in and around our space, it will affect us negatively as well. Do you ever notice that when you are frying something in your home, the smell tends to hang for quite a while? Toxic energy operates very similarly and when someone brings in negativity, it has a way of hanging in the space around you. It will absolutely have a negative effect.

Here's a question you can ask yourself. Imagine someone who is in your life that creates stress and drama in all the spaces they occupy. Perhaps it is a family member or someone who pretends to be your friend or, maybe, it is a negative coworker. Now imagine this person standing in front of you. I want you to imagine their response when you tell them "You are no longer allowed in my home." Or for the coworker, "You are no longer allowed in my office." How do you think this person will respond?

Toxic people are like an unlit match. We all know one, if not a few. They walk around and they may act calm and even caring, but in reality, we all know that at any moment, with the right type of friction, toxic people will explode much like striking a match.

Granted, this could be a caregiver, a parent, or elderly family member, a next-door neighbor, etc. You may feel completely powerless to extricate yourself from this dynamic and from their influence. However, you must understand that, like the lit match, they can't burn forever. Their hostility will eventually give way to indifference. Name-calling, gossip, and perhaps even some harassment might be the result of you enforcing your personal boundaries. All of this is to say that, for the long run, don't you believe that your peace of mind is worth the small amount of drama when extricating these individuals from your space?

Do you ever wonder why it is so difficult to allow a confrontation to take place? It is so uncomfortable to enforce our boundaries with toxic people because they are not afraid of confrontation. This is one of their choice weapons to control and influence the people in their lives. When we begin to understand that their dysfunction belongs to them and that we are not obligated to tolerate their negative behavior, we begin to make positive changes in our lives, and we become more empowered to determine how our energy is utilized.

No, of course I'm not trying to say that this process is going to be easy. It usually isn't because, typically, the toxic people that have an impact in our lives are the ones that are the closest to us. Toxic people do not have emotional profit to be toxic with total strangers, for the long run at least, or with people that are empowered to supervise them at work or otherwise have some type of emotional or financial influence upon them. Toxic people take advantage of those who have thin or nonexistent boundaries. They tend to gravitate towards personalities of people who are altruistic in nature. They are emotional vampires. Understand, that while their toxicity directed at you may feel personal, it isn't. Once you have chosen to make necessary changes in your life, you become obligated to communicate clearly to these individuals that their energy is no longer welcome. When you communicate that their behaviors are no longer allowed, you will start to feel the strength of spirit that we all have within us.

Engaging in a confrontation does not mean you are a confrontational person. Refusing to allow the toxicity of other people to affect you is a terrifying construct for the toxic person. You can have empathy for that individual because of the change you are enforcing upon your personal life but having empathy does not equal allowing the parasitic events to continue.

There are all kinds of complex relationships based upon the needs of the emotional vampire. If you are involved in a family situation, there can be many aspects and many considerations in making these changes with regards to complex family relationships. For example, if you decide that you will no longer tolerate your mother coming over to your house unannounced, you may have siblings who tolerate the same behavior from her. When you make these changes, your siblings may assert themselves in a projection of their own frustration. Perhaps they do not have the willingness or the courage to do the same with your mother. For them, it might be a simpler route to attack you for daring to enforce your own boundaries. When you refuse to tolerate your mother's behavior, she may, in fact, magnify her behavior towards your siblings which will cause them to react negatively towards you. It is important to expect this outcome. You still have a right to assert your boundaries.

Know that none of this is deserved by you. When you are kind to yourself, you have the ability to be kind to other people, while at the same time enforcing your boundaries. Name calling, judgments, and all the other toxic behaviors that are magnified to control you, are a manifestation of the fear that toxic people hold. Nothing more. It is a difficult process to extricate yourself but remember to be kind to yourself. Remember, you do not have to hold anger when you enforce your boundaries. Remember, you are responsible for your own energies, both in what you tolerate as well as what you express to the world around you.

The procession of your energy is your responsibility. You, and only you, are accountable for what you tolerate and for what you project. Meditating to find clarity is key to maintaining the direction of this effort in eradicating toxicity from your life and, as a result, from your heart and spirit.

When you are kind to yourself, anger has no room to grow. Remember, the toxic person, in their attempt to control you, will use their manipulative tactics to trigger your anger to justify their treatment of you. It is irrelevant, if in the past, you have been intolerant to toxic behaviors and have responded angrily. When you are making a change, you must start now and in the present. Understand where you have allowed these toxic projections to trigger your anger. Understand how your anger benefits the toxic person. It is important to understand how your anger serves you and how it does not serve you. Understand, that while valid, your anger may also be used against you. *If the toxic person can trigger your anger, then they are in control.* Remember that.

Practicing kindness is not easy, but it is critical as a measure of success in this evolution of eradicating toxicity. It may feel uncomfortable at first, because when our boundaries have been violated repeatedly, we are hurt, and we are traumatized. Anger is an expected result of this trauma. Practicing kindness is a diffusion of that anger and, even though you may actually feel angry, having a logical understanding of how the toxic influence from the person who seeks to control you, will help you to not demonstrate your anger thereby allowing the toxic individual to use it as a currency of control.

Being authentic does not mean that you must express your emotions to other people, particularly when these people are emotionally parasitic. You may feel anger.

Acknowledging that you are angry to yourself is all you need to do in order to be authentic, particularly when these individuals need you to express your anger so that they can control you. Behaving in a timely manner despite feeling anger is an action of boundary enforcing.

So, as an example, when you hear the doorbell, or you hear the door open at an early hour, you may say something like "I'm sorry, Mom, but we are sleeping in today. I will call you later. Here, let me help you back to your car." She may have a history of creating hysterics when she is confronted with her inappropriate behavior. She may project a victimization if her shame is triggered by your enforcement. She may make statements to elicit a sympathetic response from you. "But, I need to talk to you. Did you know that my co-worker died? Don't you even care about me?" "I'm sorry to hear your coworker died. I'll give you a call later today and we can talk about it."

Perhaps she displays cheerfulness when she perpetuates a sense of victimhood. You may feel yourself compelled to become even more angry as her behavior becomes increasingly dramatic.

Remember to be kind but to be firm. Remember you deserve to enforce your boundaries. You are obligated only to yourself by being kind and making a determination for how you are going to be treated, as well as how you treat others.

Don't forget that the toxic personality comes from a place of trauma and pain that has been unresolved in a functional way. Again, you can have empathy and understanding for these individuals, but that is not the same as tolerating their poor behavior.

Remember, in the evolution of growth of the spirit, your changes are not just about preventing other people from harming you. It is about holding yourself accountable for not harming other people as well. It is a holistic evolution that, while difficult, is wholly fulfilling and worthwhile.

CHAPTER TEN

PRIDE

Pride. What is the purpose of being prideful? When you think of someone who is prideful, what are your opinions?

There's a difference between being proud versus being prideful. I am proud of my children. I am proud of the hard work I have done, both in my personal life, as well as in my career. It's a positive aspect to have pride in one's own accomplishments. However, being prideful can be destructive in so many ways. In my practice, over the years, I have observed a variety of different manifestations of pride. Many of these clients exhibit pride as a measure of defense and protection of one's self. As always, I operate from a position of nonjudgmental stance and when I see this, I always observe it with compassion and empathy. I don't believe anyone comes into this life manifesting pride simply because they are cruel of character. I think people who are prideful do so because they feel that it is a necessary measure to protect themselves from the threat of harm.

Being prideful means lacking humility. Typically, the person who is prideful has learned this, either through observing the behavior of a caregiver, or has learned to behave in this manner to defend against humiliation.

The adult who has suffered through humiliation as a trauma, perhaps as a child, can sometimes manifest prideful behaviors as a result. The sad aspect of all of this is that the prideful person, through their own defense mechanisms, is denying the very joy they are so desperately entitled to.

Prideful behavior is malignant and affects every aspect of a person's life. When a person has unresolved traumatic humiliation and responds in prideful behavior that person categorically behaves in a way that is devoid of any compassion or empathy towards other people. They simply cannot express compassion because all their energy is tied up in the defense mechanism of prideful behavior. The pain of humiliation is like a wet blanket they carry around all the time, draped across their shoulders, coloring all their decisions in life. Prideful behavior hurts other people and carries with-it long-term implications.

When a person exhibits prideful behavior and lack of humility, there is the resistance to accountability. When there is no accountability there is no healing from the original trauma. The fear of re-traumatization and humiliation for the prideful person is so ingrained in the psyche, that there is very little room for concern with how their behavior affects other people. They are consumed with not being humiliated.

Are you a prideful person? It's OK to say yes. It's OK to say no. It's OK to say I'm not sure or I don't know. If you know that you're a prideful person, are you aware of the implications on how that affects the people around you? Better yet, ask yourself this question. "If I walked into a large gathering of people and I tripped and fell in front of them and they all pointed at me and laughed, how would I feel?" Of course, this is a metaphor but ask yourself how you would genuinely feel in that scenario. The truth is, most people would feel embarrassed and silly, regardless of whether they had humiliation as a trauma in their past. It's a normal human response to feel a bit humiliated in that type of situation. But for the person who experienced humiliation, perhaps as a child, or who was raised by a prideful person who ingrained in them certain behaviors, this experience could be deeply traumatic, triggering all kinds of anger and hostility.

A big part of transitioning from being prideful into a headspace and a spiritual awakening of growth and wellness, comes from the acknowledgment of worthiness. If a person, ideally, were to identify where their traumatic humiliation occurred and then was able to logically assess the injury that experience caused them, then that person would be able to isolate that experience and separate it from value of self. The person who is traumatized and humiliated has a feeling of low sense of self-worth based upon the experience of the humiliation itself. That trauma created a schema or a belief of a low sense of self-worth. This is a complete and total fallacy. Just because something terrible happened to you when you were little, is not a marker of your value. If you are behaving in a way that is indicative of being prideful, with an inability to accept accountability for your own behavior as an adult, then it is simply time to flip the channel from your fear-based thought process into a love-based mindset.

It's time to take a breath and close your eyes and tell yourself:

"I deserve to treat myself better. I deserve to behave in a way that is indicative of a healthy spirit and a whole sense of well-being. I deserve an opportunity to do better. I deserve an opportunity to repair the damage I have inflicted as a direct result of my own pain. I deserve to hold myself accountable as a measure of my wellness and my growth of spirit. I deserve to love myself fully and to love others with humility and vulnerability."

Being prideful is unhealthy. It is unhealthy, not because you are harmful necessarily to other people (which is a reason that it is not a good marker of self), but because it is a roadblock to your spiritual growth. You are here for a reason. You have a purpose while you are here on this earth. Align yourself with what that purpose is. Express kindness for yourself first. Express compassion for yourself. Express empathy for what you have experienced and for what others have done to you and have not made right. Know that your pride is not who you are and that you do not have to carry it any longer. Know that if you step into a social gathering and you trip and fall and know that if everyone stands around and points and laughs at you, that reflects their character and not yours. That reflects their lack of empathy, not yours. That reflects their shallowness and lack of compassion and is not an expression of your value and worthiness. You have a right to make mistakes. You have a right to not be perfect all the time. You have a right to hold space for the errors that you make in this life and to make accountable those errors that have hurt others. You do not have to carry the weight of pride around your neck like a noose. You do not have to feel humiliation when you make a mistake. You deserve to look in the mirror and express love and under-standing and kindness for yourself when other people have failed to do so.

When we complete an inventory of how we have harmed other people and we categorically act in a way that is of the intent to correct that harm our soul shines. Our heart melds together as though it were never broken to begin with. When we make amends for what we have done to other people without the expectation of forgive-ness we have done everything that we can. We have made amends regardless of whether they are accepted by those we have harmed. There is nothing else that we can do besides to change our behavior in the future. In order to receive love, we must first believe that we deserve it and we must first give it to ourselves. The greatest love of all must come from within, first and foremost. If we do not believe that we deserve good things, we will not receive them. In order to believe, we must first repair what we have damaged. In order to repair, we must acknowledge that the pain we feel is not an indication of our value.

It takes practice. It is not something that will happen overnight. Flipping your internal channel to a more positive and loving dynamic is the first step to evolving into the loving and kind and compassionate spiritual being that I know you want to be and that I know you are.

(See the chapters on accountability and worthiness for additional support in this topic.)

CHAPTER ELEVEN

CULTURAL INFLUENCE

Cultural influences deeply affect how we behave and grooms us on what we do or do not tolerate in our day to day lives.

Whether we realize it or not we are all exposed to cultural influences in some shape, form, or fashion at some, or more than one point, in our lives. I was born and raised in rural Alabama. If I had to generalize my social and communal cultural exposure and influences, it would be Southern Baptist, football, and racism. It wouldn't be until many years later, during my active duty service time in the Air Force, where I realized that I have been deeply affected by sexist cultural ideas, as well. All these influences affect how we see ourselves, how we see our self-worth, as well as what we assume other people say about us. Society tells women, for instance, be nice, cross your legs, and smile. For whatever reason, it seems like women are a commodity for the validation and encouragement of the men around them. I didn't even realize that I felt obligated to make the people around me feel better about themselves. My cultural influences ran so deep, that I felt guilty if I did not ensure that those around me were always comfortable. On a subconscious level, I would grapple with the anxiety-provoking situation of allowing other people to treat me poorly as a consequence of not being rude, often leaving the situations feeling discouraged and devalued. I was not empowered to feel OK with standing up for myself and enforcing my own personal boundaries. Through my clinical experiences with clients, I have seen this is a prevalent trend with women.

"Don't be rude!" "Be nice." Culture dictates that the worst thing in the world a woman can be, is a bitch. There are all kinds of euphemisms at the ready in social media and on TV and radio, that often isolate this concept using terms such as "resting bitch face."

Why is resting bitch face a thing? Why does it carry a tone of negativity to have a face that is indicative of bitchiness? Why does this have to be negative and why does it have to be attributed to just women?

The cultural implications of grooming women to believe that their worth is wrapped up in how they make other people feel, is a major factor that causes chronic depression and anxiety in women.

When people are not given the tools and the skills and the empowerment necessary for self-actualization, the result is a long-standing chronic issue of negative self-worth.

These cultural influences are not just isolated with women, however. Men are told, as little boys, to be strong and to fix things and to know things. Don't ask for help and don't show vulnerability, because that means you're weak. Men must face incredible odds as they grow up in deciphering what it means to be a man, based upon the cultural influences that they are groomed with.

You might be surprised to learn men are affected by cultural influences just as much as women.

In Western culture, it is considered poor form for men to express vulnerability, tearfulness, or anything remotely feminine. It is interpreted as an expression of emotional weakness, which is predominately frowned upon, universally in the West. It is as though being feminine is seen as a negative context. Speaking generally, western culture dictates that men must always be strong. If a man were to express anything personal or to outwardly express his deepest emotions, he would simply be judged as not being worthy or masculine. Little boys are groomed to play rough, learn a trade, fix a car, shoot a gun, and to never ask for help. There is truth in the fact men don't ask for directions. It's simply because culture has implicated them as being weak if they do so. When we take away the cultural influences that are negative and shame inducing, we can cultivate a newness and an openness in our lives with love and longing and growth. When we do not adhere these social norms and the cultural grooming, we hold space for ourselves to determine our own sensibilities and our own value systems. We become accountable for what we think, based upon what is important to us as individuals and not to society. It is absolutely a process and not something that comes freely and easily for most people, but it can happen! A big part of cultural cognitive rebalancing is to compare different cultures and understanding the nuances that make them valuable to the cultures they represent. For example, in many Middle Eastern cultures, it is considered quite normal, and sometimes expected, for men to hold hands while having a conversation. When we think about that in the lens of western dynamics, it seems a bit off putting and almost homosexual, which is, again, counterintuitive toward the western culture dynamic of heteronormative viewpoints which magnify the worthiness of the straight male and minimize, and often demonizes, the worth of women, femininity, and homosexuality.

It's just a game. Western culture is an idea and nothing more about what it means to be a woman or a man. It's when those ideals run counter to the interpersonal value system of an individual is when you have distress. When these cultural value systems place value for a mindset or dogma over the value system of a different dynamic, that is the root of social dysfunction.

I truly believe when we as a society, collectively, gather and hold ourselves accountable for conducting our own interpersonal investigations on what we appreciate and what we value, only then will we be able to disassemble the institutionalized grooming construct of what is and is not appropriate behavior, culturally speaking.

It's hard to turn your back on a cultural ideal that dictates what you should or should not believe, because the cultural ideal eliminates the need to engage in critical thinking on your behalf.

It makes it easier to heft the weight of responsibility of independent thought towards a universally accepted ideal, no matter how wrong it may be or what group or groups of people may be adversely affected.

If someone hands me an idea and says this is the way things should work then as a human being I might naturally want to adopt that ideal as a measure of not having to do any additional work on my own. Dogma has a way of providing the "answers" for people.

Culture is not always a bad, fear-based construct. Often, it is a representation of heritage and history for a group of people to maintain throughout time to ensure that the legacy of their people is not forgotten. Have you ever traveled to a different country and noticed different symbols, art, architecture, and especially the food they eat as being a marker of their pride in their heritage? This is a demonstration of culture based in love for their people. When culture is used to control society, that is a fear-based concept and, like all things, must be taken into consideration for everyone.

Ultimately, your schoolteacher was right. *You just need to do your homework.*

You do not necessarily have to disagree with the cultural influences that you were groomed with, but you won't know that until you actually take the time to identify your own value system and how that lines up with the cultural influences in your world.

CHAPTER TWELVE

LOVE

One thing is absolutely for certain. It is critical for us to experience love as human beings. When we are born into this world and are not given an opportunity to experience love in a healthy and non-shameful dynamic, we simply have no ability to understand how it is supposed to feel. We must have the demonstration in our lives and when we don't, we are not able to meet our potential as a loving person participating in the human experience.

I have often said you never fully understand vulnerability until you have a child. The truth is also, that you do not fully understand love until you have a child. Before I go any further, I do want to say that people who do not have children absolutely experience love. People who don't have children can experience profound and deeply rewarding love of self as well as in relationships with others. I am relating my own personal experience, as I did not fully grasp the weight of what love truly meant until I had a baby.

My son was conceived during a relationship with someone I thought that I was in love with. All my life and my entire world at understanding what it meant to be here and who I was as a person, was completely obliterated the moment I gave birth. My understanding of love continued to evolve as the days, weeks, and months went on. I was his sole caregiver, as his birth father was uninterested in raising a child. The responsibility was not lost on me and the gravity of how important it was to not fail him was huge beyond measure. As someone who experienced the consistency of feeling emotionally neglected as a child, it was not lost on me that I felt an incredible responsibility to not fail my son in the ways that I felt I had been failed.

Moreover, looking at him and realizing that even though I felt broken, less than, and unworthy as a person, I began to realize that this tiny child did not share my beliefs. His eyes and his smile would light up a room and he demonstrated this when he saw me. When I would walk into daycare to pick him up, his beautiful cherub face, framed by his blonde locks of hair, would explode in a jubilant grin. He did this as a baby, and it continued throughout toddlerhood and preschool on into kindergarten. I could not fail him. It simply was not an option. His happiness in seeing me was validation that I had to be doing something right as his mother. He consistently demonstrated unconditional love for me and, looking back, I realize that he was teaching me what it meant to love someone. I was also learning how to love unconditionally. We were teaching each other.

Through this experience, it was unavoidable to make the assertion that I had to take better care of myself for my son. It was always for him. When he was little, it was not on my radar to take care of myself simply because I deserve to take care of myself. It was such a foreign concept at the time, because it had never been consistently demonstrated by anyone in my life. From that perspective, everything I did was for my son because I love him.

*I didn't know that I **could** love myself.*

I didn't know I should love myself. All I knew at the time was that this little guy depended on me for everything and I was able to either repeat my past or create a new future for him by giving him everything I never had in the way of encouragement and support. Oh, I was not perfect by any stretch of the imagination. I made mistakes. I got tired and I allowed my exhaustion to color my tone of voice and demonstrate irritation in dealing with him from time to time, as most parents do. I never really identified what kind of discipline I wanted to use or how to implement appropriate discipline. I had no clue how to discipline a two-year-old. I didn't know what the appropriate ways were to change poor behavior. All I had to go on were my own experiences with my dysfunctional and abusive childhood. Throughout all of this though, the recurring theme was love. It was suffocating for me at times, because I loved him so much that I would struggle at work with worry, anxiety, and concern about whether he was being mistreated by his caregivers at daycare. I was on a very tight income and was paying for childcare on my own, despite struggling to secure some type of financial support from his birth father. He was not always afforded the most ideal childcare situations while I was working. I remember the first day I started a new job when he was only six weeks old and he was just barely old enough to start going to daycare. The only daycare that had room for him was a 30-mile round-trip out of my way on my way to work. I remember the first day of dropping off my newborn baby to a group of ladies who were kind and reassuring that he would be just fine, and they would take great care of him. I cried in the car all the way to my first day on the job. It was as though there was a rubber band connected between his little tiny heart and mine and the further I drove the tighter and tighter that rubber band got and it pulled and tugged at my heart in ways that made me scared I would fall apart at work. I simply could not come unglued on my first day of the job I had just secured, and I needed so desperately to take care of the both of us. I wanted to be with my baby. My breasts ached to nurse him, but I did not have a breast pump and, due to my work schedule and lack of additional support, chose to bottle feed him because it just wasn't working with my schedule.

So, I made the drive and ultimately, overtime, found a new daycare that was on the way to my work and that provided an enormous reprieve on the significant amount of anxiety I was dealing with daily.

I missed my baby during my workdays.

The connection I felt to my child during my workday when I was away from him was a feeling that, to this day, I struggle to describe.

If I had such a hard time finding love and compassion for myself, how is it I found a seemingly bottomless chasm of love for a child that I bore? Logic dictates that if you don't love yourself, how can you love a child you brought into the world?

This is a question that I always felt was pressing and one that I investigated on a routine basis. This was a part of my evolution of understanding that my need for love and my need for healing and growth ultimately started with the understanding that I deserve just as much as my baby does. In fact, it was from this experience of being a mother that drove me into identifying compassion for myself with the realization that I should take care of myself because my son deserves it and because I deserve it.

It is irrelevant whether you have children to the fact that you deserve love. It is also irrelevant to the fact as to whether you feel lovable. The truth is, that in order to heal from anything, love must be the key component. Love is the result of doing all this work in finding yourself. You have to turn the light switch on to make the room brighter. You have the power to illuminate your life with self-love. No one else can truly love you until you understand your own worth. Your wellbeing is internal and other people recognize this, whether its intentional on their part or not. When you realize what you're worth it is impossible to tolerate less than what you deserve. When you hold space for yourself and grace for your errors, you express a kindness and compassion for yourself that is undeniable. Throughout this lifelong journey, you learn how to let go of those old schemas and ways of thinking. You let go of the dysfunctional attitudes and behaviors exhibited to you by caregivers. You send negative and toxic energy back to where it came from, replacing this vacancy with love and gratitude.

You also get to heal and, therefore, open yourself up to love. All positive emotions come from the basic emotion of love.

I love you.

Love is a verb. Love is an action. Love is intentional.

We value love as though it is this scarce, fragile thing. Love is scarce only because we choose to be selective with who we express love to. Love is fragile only because we treat it that way. In fact, love is the strongest emotion there is. It is anything but fragile and that's why it scares us. We want and need love so desperately in our lives, that we ration the amount that we express to others.

What we don't realize is that everyone else is doing the same thing. We withhold love as currency, as a measure of control in relationships. What happens is that when we do that, love simply dies. If love is not expressed openly and without reservation, then it ceases to exist as it is no longer love. That is why in abusive, gaslighting relationships many things are called love, but they really aren't. Control, approval, validation, and manipulation is all masked under the veil of "love", but it's just the manifestation of fear-based thinking by individuals who cannot conceive of love in its authentic form, so they counterfeit it with people who are equally desperate. The same goes for familial relationships between parent / child, etc. Love is often counterfeit and sold under a variety of monikers to entice the broken to acquiesce to the desires of the abuser.

Real love.

Have you ever experienced real, genuine, unrestrained, unconditional love? Perhaps you have not experienced this from someone else. It's ok if you haven't. It doesn't matter if you haven't. Love comes from within.

Stay with me.

I love you.

That's right.

I love you.

Me, the author of this book. I am expressing love for you, the reader. I have no knowledge of who you are, where you come from or what kind of person you are. It's irrelevant.

I choose to express love. It's my choice.

Expressing love is like lighting a candle from another candle. It takes absolutely nothing away from a candle to light another candle. It takes nothing away from me, the writer, to express love to you, the reader. I don't have to know who you are to express love.

I love you because I choose to.

Love is absolutely that simple. We have been groomed to withhold love because we have been told it's scary to love someone who may not love you back.

You don't have to expect anything to love someone.

You don't have to receive love in order to give it to someone else.

When we express love for others we grow love in abundance for ourselves.

The other day I was driving home from work and a driver cut in front of me causing me to slam on my brakes. In the past, (I'll be honest it hasn't been that long ago, but I'm growing too) this situation would have caused me to release a stream of expletives. However, once I got my heart rate down, I expressed love for that driver. I honestly didn't feel it at first, but I reiterated the sentiment. "I love you." My response to this situation evolved from a sympathetic nervous response (fight, flight or freeze) to a para-sympathetic nervous response. (recovery/feed/breed/calm), "I love you," I repeated until I was completely calm.

When we express love for other people, there is no room for hostility. Love wins when we let it. When we express love, we must take note that we are allowing ourselves to be vulnerable to our own willingness to connect. You see, that's the fear we have. We fear that we aren't loveable. We fear that others will see the brokenness that we feel inside ourselves and we are scared that if we express love that the love will not be returned. The important thing to remember here is that it doesn't matter if the love is not returned. You are not broken. You do not have to receive love to give love. Love is boundless and resides limitlessly within all of us. Just because you may not have experienced receiving real, authentic, genuine love from someone doesn't mean that you cannot express real, authentic, and genuine love for someone.

You are influential beyond measure. Your only limit is what you believe. Most of us have been programmed to believe that we must restrict our expression of love as a measure of being authentic in a relationship. Can you imagine going on a date with someone and having them say "I love you" before the main course at dinner arrives? That's a terrifying prospect. It carries so much weight to it because we have been programmed to believe that.

Looking at this situation logically there are two possibilities: One, this person that you're on a date with is a genuine, loving and kind person who believes that love is a boundless commodity and treats everyone they meet with an act of genuine loving kindness. When this person says "I love you," they mean it with every fiber of their being. The only difference is that going on the date is an interview for a potential partnership based in a loving connection. Or, two, this person is socially inept and doesn't understand the social contracts surrounding the expression of love too early in the courting experience. The sad part is that the person who doesn't understand social dynamics likely doesn't have a full appreciation of the expression of love and is only making this expression out of some sense of obligatory engagement to secure a partner. The latter, of course, is something that should be alarming to most people, but being lonely will cause us to make excuses for other people's behavior. I've been there a few times, myself.

Why is it so scary to express love?

Who do you love?

When you are angry or upset with someone you love, do you feel a hesitation in expression of love for them?

Do you use love and validation as a reward in relationships when the other party participates in the relationship to your liking?

How do you express love for someone?

How has love been expressed to you?

Cultural influences and social norms have created a template that we blindly follow with regards to how we express love. It unnecessarily causes grief and pain for individuals who desperately want to receive love. Perhaps we are fearful that we would inadvertently create an unwelcome attachment from someone who misinterprets our expression. You don't have to want to spend your life in a partnership with someone in order to express love for that person. Unfortunately, many people may be confused with the expression of love as meaning that they are the ONLY person that you love.

Expressing love for others can be achieved beyond words. You don't necessarily have to say the words "I love you" to express love. In fact, it's preferable to demonstrate loving acts towards and for other people instead of making a culturally implicating statement such as "I love you."

Individuals caught up in dysfunctional relationships will often ignore red flags, such as gaslighting and controlling behavior in others, simply because the other party will state "I love you," even though they never make attempts to demonstrate love through authentic means.

Real love is never restrained. It is never withheld. It is always upfront and authentic. If you can be truly honest with yourself, you know when love is genuine and when it isn't.

Do you love yourself?

Do you want to love yourself?

Do you deserve love?

Do others deserve to be loved by you?

Love is the one resource that lives in abundance within all of us, but is the one commodity we find the hardest to tap into. You have infinite love resources. You have the capacity to love deeply and without reservation. When you are ready and when you choose, you can express love that is immeasurable. You can express love for yourself, your family, your friends, your enemies etc. You can break free of cultural restrictions. You have the right and the ability to express your love the way you choose to do so.

Do you know how to love others?

Does loving someone scare you?

For folks like me, people raised in fear-based thinking patterns, the expression of love is sometimes the only thing that we have control over. So, if you can imagine a child in an abusive environment feeling completely out of control, being able to decide on when to express love is the only conduit of feeling some sense of influence in an environment of tyranny. When a child is raised like this, it feels impossible to be vulnerable to our own capacity for loving others. It's terrifying, in fact, to think that we could express love for someone else when all we know is that it would be used against us or would be considered a form of weakness. When a child is terrorized by the very people that are expected to express unconditional love, then it's only natural to expect the child to distrust any connection with someone who professes love. For me, it was reiterated many times in future relationships that I was "loveable". Logically, now, I can assert the dynamics of these relationships as having ended for a variety of reasons, none of which had anything to do with my worthiness of self or being a lovable person. Of course, at the time I didn't know this, and these experiences only served to reinforce my belief of not being loveable or of not deserving love.

I love me.

I love who I am. I love my growth as a person. I love everything about me including my flaws. They make me who I am. I love the work I do both in my personal life and in my professional life.

It is in this discovery of my own love of self where I have identified my worth. I know what I am worth and, as a result, I have a keen understanding of what I deserve in my relationships with others. I understand and identify fear-based thinking and when I encounter that in others, particularly when it's negatively projected towards me, I simply send it away in love. I hold space for my worth and my growth. While unfortunate for others, sometimes those individuals are at a different place in life and project their own dysfunction. It's ok when this happens. You must simply enforce boundaries, recognize the behavior, express your own refusal to tolerate it and return to sender. You do all this with love, both for the other person as well as for yourself.

It's not a perfect process by any measure. We are all human beings and fallible by nature. It pisses us off when we express love for someone and then it's mishandled or misused. No one wants that. No one wants to express love for someone and then have that love manipulated. It's part of life.

Do you love someone who refuses to accept your love?

Do you carry a torch for someone who refuses to give you time? Should you still love that person?

I say "Yes" and here's why. If you express love for someone that is not returned or is not accepted, remember what your reason is for expression of love in the first place. You express love just because. There's no quid pro quo when it comes to love, it just is. If your heart hurts because you love someone who doesn't accept your love or doesn't return it, then you've got to take some time to figure out why you're allowing this pain to begin with.

I had the biggest crush on this guy in high school and for a short while after. We never really "dated," but I loved him deeply. He was my first and I thought that I wanted to spend my life with him at the time. Looking back, he never gave me any indication that he felt remotely the same toward me. He never agreed to be my boyfriend. I was the aggressor and willingly volunteered my virginity to him. He was funny and kind. He wasn't a mean person at all. We had a great time when we worked together at the fast food restaurant. I poured all the love I had into creating something with him that simply never happened. I got hurt because I hurt myself. I loved him and thought that if I loved him hard enough, he would love me back. It didn't happen and for many years I was resentful towards him, even though I acted friendly. He never made any promises to me and, as the years went on, I realized that it was just my own child-like adoration of someone who made me laugh. Because I never witnessed a healthy relationship, I had no foundation of what to expect. When he went out of his way to make me laugh, I must have assumed that he liked me. I'm sure he felt some form of validation in making me laugh. It felt good to be around him because of this and I mistook that for a perceived romantic interest on his part. Maybe he was interested at one point, but due to my willingness to have sex with him, was a bit overwhelming for him? I don't know. I just remember t I thought loving him as hard as I could would result in my feeling loved back. That didn't happen.

I did not love myself back then.

I did not have the ability to understand how to love, respect, and hold a space of worthiness for myself just because I had no idea that I should do so. Even though, in my teenage years, my homelife improved greatly, (I began defending myself against the physical assaults and as a result they stopped, though they manifested as increased emotional abuse.), I was still sort of floating about in the aftermath. I was clueless on how relationships worked and had no idea about what it meant to have self-respect or a sense of wellness. It was like I had been blown off a sinking ship. The ship was gone below the seas, but I was still floating about in the refuse and debris of the past. I was merely surviving. I didn't know what else to do or if there was anything else to do.

I smile when I think back now on that love-starved, 17-year-old with the knock-knees and the freckles. I can see her now with her brunette hair teased and sprayed with her work visor neatly perched in the nest of 90s mall hair. I see her giggle when her friends come through the drive thru and cut up on those hot Alabama summer nights. She's adorable with her uniform sprayed with oil and salt from the fry machine. On the inside, she's an angry, hurt, and sensitive mess, but on the outside, she's a beautiful, funny, smart, intuitive and creative young woman who has absolutely no idea what phenomenal things lie in wait in her future.

I love her. I love me.

Can you imagine yourself this way?

Can you step outside of yourself and see yourself
with the kindness, beauty and love that you deserve?

Describe yourself through this lens.

Who do you dare to love?

CHAPTER THIRTEEN

HONESTY

Remember, the purpose is not to find judgment or blame, but to find reasons for the dysfunctional logic that causes us to make poor decisions.

When was the last time you told a lie?

Perhaps you don't remember. Perhaps you don't remember the last time you willingly sacrificed the truth for a more palatable, albeit false, scenario. It's OK if this topic makes you a little bit uncomfortable. The discomfort you feel is the result of having a consciousness that desires equanimity, fairness, and a life of authenticity. If you are someone who uses deception and manipulation to function in your day-to-day activities and you do not feel any sense of discomfort then that could be the result of many different reasons. If you choose to continue reading, I think that is enough demonstration of willful honest intent for making positive change.

Perhaps you are someone who survives through the creation of your own reality. I have to say, there is something commendable about a person who is resourceful to the point of creating a fantasy as a bridge to survive this life. Unfortunately, what happens when we create a fallacy or a story is we become aligned with that creation in a way that places us in a situation where we must continually make a choice to either continue the fantasy or to admit that it was the creation of our imagination. Our ego does not like to be wrong. If we create a story of fantasy and then perpetuate that narrative as though it is authentic and real, we become slaves to the fantasy, that is until we are aware enough of self to take a step forward into reality and to learn how to wholly accept the truth of our decisions.

Is there an aspect of your life you have perpetuated as the truth when, in actuality, it was a creation that you sold as a measure to make yourself feel more acceptable or lovable to others?

Instead of holding safe boundaries for yourself when people press you for intimate details about your life, do you give them a falsehood as opposed to confronting them about the inappropriate nature of their intrusion? For example: "I heard you were engaged again. That's nice. How many times have you been married by the way?" Would you answer truthfully and then feel embarrassed or ashamed if you have not been comfortable giving that information? Would you tell that person "I'm not sure what the number of my previous marriages has to do with my engagement but thank you for congratulating me. I'll be sure to pass on your sentiments to my fiancé." Maybe you might go the more direct route with a comment such as "My previous marriages are in the past and certainly none of your business.", or would you avoid the question altogether or lie about the answer?

The purpose of this chapter is not necessarily to identify where you are lying to other people. It is, however, an opportunity to identify how we relate to other people with regards to how we see ourselves. If we are uncomfortable with certain dynamics about our lives, we may not feel comfortable sharing those details with other people. Additionally, we may feel intimidated when other people express an interest in our lives and want to impress people by giving details that are inaccurate or deliberately incorrect.

We certainly do not owe all the intimate details of our personal lives and our personal narrative to other people, especially when it makes us uncomfortable sharing these details. The problems come from feeling as though we are not worthy to enforce boundaries. Sometimes, it just feels better to be deceptive with others rather than expose our authentic selves.

If you have issues, stories, situations, that are a part of your authentic history in narrative that you are not comfortable sharing with other people, then you do not have to share those details. There's absolutely nothing wrong with enforcing boundaries regarding information about your past traumas, embarrassing situations, etc.

It is important to understand how lies can erode our sense of well-being. Not all lies are harmful. If we meet someone on the street and ask for directions and comment that the city that we are currently lost in is "the most beautiful place we've ever been," it is not typically a harmful deception. It is important to understand the difference between what is harmful and what is not.

The buildup.

When we create a narrative that is inaccurate or inauthentic, we create a foundation that we must build upon. Whether that is commentary shared at a family reunion about a promotion at work or how well a child is doing in school; perhaps an utterance made during a lunch break at work about buying a new home or gossiping about a fellow coworker etc. These lies become just like living breathing organisms that you must consistently feed with more lies.

Do you have lies that you feed?

It seems virtually impossible to extricate yourself from the fantasy that you have created and walk away feeling whole and respected by the people that you initially lied to.

You don't need to worry about being respected by those people. The only person who matters in this scenario is you and your respect for yourself.

It is not the end of the world to admit fault to the individuals that you shared a deceitful narrative with. Taking accountability and ownership for your behavior and your actions is all that is necessary in this process. Going into this action of accountability is incredibly courageous because there will always be people who will seek to judge and blame. There will always be people who will find fault and use your narrative against you.

Do it anyway.

Take your power back.

Stop feeding those little lie-gremlins that you created from a fear-based thinking mindset.

The judgment that you receive from others is irrelevant to your healing.

I understand your lies may have caused others pain and confusion. It is your responsibility to accept this as part of your healing and growth. Taking ownership for the insult and injury you have caused through your own trauma-induced behaviors is critical to your wellness. Their judgment of you through their pain is not going to kill you.

Accept this with love and compassion and kindness for yourself, as well as for those you have harmed.

This process will eradicate the buildup of deceit and betrayal in the lives that you have been investing your energy into. This energy can now be freed up to be focused into a love-based mindset geared towards, not only healing of yourself, but encouraging and inspiring others to do the same.

Naturally, of course, this process does not occur overnight, but your thought process can change quickly. Once you realize there is a mess to be cleaned up you will feel freer and will start acting in a love-based growth mindset. You will learn to expect and accept the judgment and you will learn to be OK with that. You will learn that anyone who harbors negative feedback or judgment and blame for you, is doing so out of their own pain or their projection of pain toward you. Remember to always accept only what you need to as a measure of accountability and to enforce healthy boundaries against that which you do not.

Dealing with liars

Do you tolerate being lied to?

Do you hesitate calling people out when you know they are feeding you a line?

When you know you're being lied to, how does it make you feel?   _

When you discover someone has been lying to you, how do you handle it?

Why do you think people lie to you?

The first year I was on active duty in the Air Force, I met this guy who really made me feel special. I was 21 and still heartbroken from the breakup prior to my enlistment. I never thought that I would ever feel a connection that strongly ever again as most youngsters do. He was unfailingly charismatic, an amazing dancer, and kept me laughing all the time. I once even mentioned how I was saving up money to buy a bicycle. The next day, he shows up to my dorm room with a brand new 10 speed. We spent countless nights doing what young adults do when given privacy and alone time. It was thrilling. I felt beautiful and loved and whole. One day while he was at work, I went to his dorm room to surprise him when he returned from his shift. I was getting ready to go on leave for two weeks for my sister's wedding and wanted to spend as much time as possible with him before my departure. While waiting for him, I started to snoop through his wall locker and found a receipt from a jewelry store for a diamond ring. Not sure why I started snooping to begin with. I was completely shocked. I knew that I wanted to marry this guy, but I had no idea that our relationship was moving that fast. I made sure to put the receipt back exactly where I found it and took measures to calm myself down. He returned from work that day, quite unceremoniously, considering what I had recently discovered. In fact, he seemed somewhat "off". He took me to the airport the following day and promised to take care of my car for me while I was gone. Upon my return two weeks later, he met me at the airport in my vehicle, which he had personally detailed inside and out, and presented me with a bouquet of roses and a bottle of wine. We picked up immediately where we had left off two weeks prior. He didn't leave any clues or indications that he was thinking about marriage. While it was driving me nuts, I certainly did not feel entitled to address the issue or to ask him what was going on. I just assumed I would sit and wait for him to ask me. Looking back, I am certain that I assumed his demeanor was due to his nervousness in asking me to marry him and nothing more. He and I did the same work, but, because our relationship was well known, flight leadership was determined to keep us separate during our workday. On this one, particular, day I knew where he had been working and what the phone number was. Each time I attempted to call him, his coworker would tell me that he was busy and would call me back, which he never did. At the end of our shift, we were picked up in a van and taken back to the armory to turn in our firearms. On this day, the van was noticeably late in picking us up. I asked my flight Sergeant why they were so late picking us up. He said he would talk to me later about it. My frustration was rising. We arrive to the armory and, as I get downstairs, I can see my boyfriend all the way at the end of the hallway. I yelled out to him, but he ignored me and went out the side door. I attempted to follow him, but my flight sergeant reached out and stopped me and stated that he needed to talk to me. I told my flight sergeant I would talk to him later and that I need to catch up with my boyfriend. He continued to block my egress and stated, "That's why I need to talk to you." Again, so much confusion. My flight chief walked me out of the armory and, as we were walking tried to explain to me my boyfriend was going to talk to me later and he wanted to make sure that I was up for a very deep conversation. I tried to press him to get more details, but he refused to budge and stated only that my boyfriend would have to give me those details. I immediately made my way to my boyfriend's dorm room. I pounded heavily on his door while yelling

"I know you're in there! What is going on?!" He answered the door and had clearly been crying.

His entire dorm room was covered with used tissues. I was horrified and my mind was racing. Something is definitely wrong. I sat down beside him on his bed and put my arm around him. I wanted to comfort him, as he was clearly in profound distress. I reassured him, "what is it? What is going on? I can help you. I love you." He simply looked up at me with his tear stained eyes and runny nose and said, "She's pregnant." "Who's pregnant?" "My ex."

Over the next couple of hours, he proceeded to spin a tail that encompassed terms such as "delayed pregnancy". He tried to convince me he had not actually cheated on me during my trip for my sister's wedding but, instead, wanted me to believe that a sexual encounter he had with her before we get together resulted in a "delayed pregnancy". Unbelievable. He was spinning out of control with his deceit.

"I thought you were going to propose to me." I blurted this out without thinking. My mind was racing and everything was a blur. He just stared at me blankly. "Why did you think that?" I explained to him that I had been snooping and found the receipt from the jewelry store in his wall locker before I had traveled back home for the wedding.

Then it hit me. He wasn't cheating on me. He hadn't been cheating on me at all. He was cheating on her *with me*. The ring was never meant for me. It was for her. She was his high school sweetheart and he'd told me many times they were over. This came up several times, as she routinely requested entry onto the air force base to visit him. She had even, innocently enough, approached me requesting a visitor pass. At the time, I actually felt sorry for her. I felt like a fool. I felt like I was going to throw up.

I stood up and walked out of his room without any words. I had been rattled to my core. It's the numbness I remember now. I had actually been able to step out of my emotional headspace and I pushed that piece of pain so deep, I didn't address it for many years. I avoided him from that point on, at all cost. It was difficult as we lived in the same dormitory and, from time to time, we would pass each other, either in our cars driving in opposite directions, or we'd see each other from afar. He tried to wave at me a couple of times. I pretended not to notice even though I would go to my room and cry afterwards. One day, I realized that he wasn't in the dorms anymore. Friends and co-workers told me that he'd married her and that they just had a baby. Good riddance.

His deceit and betrayal affected me deeply and still resonates with me today. However, I understand now his need to lie had absolutely nothing to do with me but, instead, came from a deeply rooted sense of pain and lack of worthiness on his part.

Not that I would have ever considered committing that level of betrayal in a relationship, I can attest that this experience and the pain that it left me with certainly inoculated me from ever lying to a potential partner.

Has anyone ever lied to you and hurt you so deeply it changed the way you think?

Do you maintain relationships and or contact with people that you know are dishonest?

Do you have family members that lie regularly to you and to other people, but because they are relatives you tolerate this behavior?

It is completely up to you to determine your sense of value when it comes to honesty. It is important, as a part of your own wellness and your own evolution to your spiritual growth, to identify what is important to you with regards to honesty. There is no black-and-white, right or wrong template to determine how to move forward in these dynamics with yourself and others. It is, however, critical to explore consciously where your values are and to align yourself with those values as a measure of healing.

CHAPTER FOURTEEN

HUMILITY

The key to making positive and permanent change in our lives is to accept our weaknesses as part of our authentic selves, willfully and honestly, with kindness and compassion.

Humility is the root word of humiliation, however, the two are vastly different concepts.

Humility is the opposite of pride.

What does it mean to you to have humility?

How do you demonstrate humility in your day-to-day activities?

Do you find it difficult to express humility?

Do you feel that when you are humble that you are overly vulnerable to attack and judgment from others?

The practice of mindfulness cultivates love-based emotional responses. When we respond to our environment from a place of love, then it is only natural for us to respond with humility. When we are humble, we respond to others and to interactions within our environment in a way that is open and accepting, without judgment or blame.

Bear in mind, transitioning from fear-based thinking and prideful behavior is difficult when it is your automatic response. Anyone who has been groomed to feel attacked or placed in a position of unworthiness will naturally respond to this dynamic with unease and trepidation. It is important to realize that just because a person lacks humility, does not indicate a lack of character or low personal morals and ethics. It is an indication of someone who has been groomed to believe that they must respond to their environment with fear-based thinking. Nothing more. It's worth stating, as well, that individuals who regularly function without humility could very well be doing it only because they have never been demonstrated positive and affirming ways of interaction with others. This can absolutely tie into cultural influences in determining how a person should or should not interact with other people. The lesson here is that when we know better, we do better. If cultural influences have dictated that a person should value another group of people less than themselves, then that is a thinking error that should be remedied. We are all products of our environment, good and bad alike.

Are you a humble person?

Do you struggle with prideful behavior and lack of humility?

Do you think that being humble equals being weak?

If lack of humility is something you are struggling with, what are the reasons for this struggle? Are they cultural? Do you have toxic influences in your life that bear judgment and blame projected at you for trying to make positive changes in your life and in how you think and feel?

Remember, each day that you are afforded here on this planet is an opportunity to start anew.

Are you who you want to be? If not, why?

You deserve the inspiration to grow and change and evolve just as much as you hold the responsibility to be humble and vulnerable to your environment.

This is all true simply because your worth is intangible and implicit, all because you are here. Your humility is an extension of our mutual consciousness and collective humanity, directed in love at yourself, as well as others. Humility is strength, not weakness.

CHAPTER FIFTEEN

FORGIVENESS

Most of us have been told, at one point or another, that forgiveness is essential to living a full and happy life. We may understand this logically, but forgiveness itself is difficult to come by when we are still hurting.

When I was an adolescent, I began to keep a diary. It was a book that did not have a lock, or any kind of security affixed to it, but merely a hardback cover with a series of blank lined pages. I believe I was around 14 years old when I started to document my feelings. Occasionally, the entries would involve some petty misunderstanding with a friend or two. Often, it was the normal dramatic interactions of young teenage girls. However, there were passages in my diary that were filled with anger and darkness directed at my father. Looking back on these pages, I see a child starving for affection and approval and validation. Looking through the pages of this old diary through my wiser clinical lens, I can remember clearly the grip of addiction that my father had to come to. I know now that he suffered immeasurable emotional pain throughout his entire life up until his death. This pain created a need for a numbing agent. He used a variety of substances to satiate his agony. Understandably, anyone who is under the influence of a substance is not going to have the capacity to provide the nurturing love towards their children. I see that now. I can even express compassion for him and what he was dealing with. I can say without hesitation I am quite proud of my own emotional growth and evolution and being able to recognize logically the reasons behind my father's neglect as well as his regular sadistic abuse of me and my siblings.

"I wish he would die. I would go to his funeral and put a dead daisy on top of his casket. I would flip him the bird and walk out," wrote a then angry 15-year-old version of myself. While I do not remember what it was that caused me to make that entry, I can safely assume that he had angrily beat me with a leather strap for some benign excuse. I wasn't a bad kid. I was a normal kid who got into normal things. I most certainly never deserved any of the physical abuse that I received. Neither did my siblings. Having been a parent myself, I am all-too familiar of being angry at my child while sober. I never physically abused my children, but I do recall the unrelenting frustration of not being able to adequately correct their behavior. As far as my father was concerned, I assume, that in his inebriated state, his rage fueled by his own trauma was the catalyst that justified his abuse, in his mind, at least.

For me, it has taken many years for me to remove my emotional response from my abuse and to be able to articulate my experiences, without judgment, in a logical frame of mind. The truth is, while I did not deserve any of his mal-treatment, I also recognize I did not receive this abuse as a merit of my own character. I was simply there, and therefore, a target.

As time moved on and as I grew into adulthood and moved away, my experiences and my relationships with others were colored by my trauma. While at times my own anger became a crutch, I can look back and be grateful for the growth and understanding I achieved through these painful experiences.

As I attempted to maintain and or reconnect with my parents, it became apparent that my father's addiction and my mother's willful and blind adoration and delusion was simply too toxic for me to allow. My father had his single engine pilot's license and, while high on opiates, would operate an aircraft. He took my young son and flew him across several states lines many years ago, unbeknownst to me until after their arrival and subsequent phone call. I attempted to resolve this issue and achieve a sense of boundaries, but was unsuccessful, as my father was simply unwilling to abide by any rules that were not his own. Therefore, I chose to disconnect all contact from my father. He would respond to my efforts by preventing my mother from interacting with me. I received an enormous amount of backlash from family and friends, who could not understand how I could cut my parents out of my life. I didn't understand why they didn't support me. In fact, the only people who truly understood what I have been dealing with and respected my decision was but a small handful of close friends, as well as my then husband.

Disconnecting from my parents was one of the most difficult and, yet, most empowering decisions I have ever made. I simply refused to allow their toxic behavior to be a negative influence. I refused to maintain any contact due to their unwillingness to be respectful of my wishes. It is not something that I would ever wish for anyone to have to go through. However, we simply cannot control the actions of other people. We can only control our response to their actions.

Regardless of what they may have thought of me at the time, I genuinely always wanted the best for them. In fact, for many years after our estrangement, I often wished that both of my parents would seek therapy and would understand and respect my feelings. I was hopeful that my father would find some help with his addiction and that my mother would be able to be honest with herself.

I began to dig in and do some real introspective work on myself with a therapist. I learned a lot about how I had been responding to others as a result of my own trauma. At one point, I felt comfortable enough to send a message to my mother on Facebook, indicating to her that I had forgiven her as well as my father. Her response to me was "we can't accept your forgiveness if we haven't done anything wrong."

Communication with my mother always felt like when you're standing next to a fan that is on high and you take your finger and slip it through the metal slats and dare yourself to allow the blades to make contact. You never know if it's going to hurt or if it's just going to surprise you a bit.

When my father died, I cried. It took a couple days after I received the news, but I did take time to invest in allowing my feelings to manifest in an authentic way. At first the tears came and then, I felt angry. The anger was different this time though. The anger I had was more about my disappointment with my father and him not trying harder. As a mother, I would do anything for my children. My children have enraged me at times, but my love for them transcends all boundaries. My children mean more to me than anyone or anything. My anger towards my father dissipated and transitioned into pity. The love I have for my children is something that has saved my life on many occasions. In the depths of despair, the only light at the end of the tunnel was the love of my children and their love for me. So, when my father died, I didn't understand how he could not try harder.

He wasn't a bad person. He had darkness in him. Human beings need connection like we need oxygen. My father never had that. My mother was the closest thing he had to unconditional love in his life and even that wasn't enough. If you never saw the color green, no one would be able to describe it to you. My father never knew love as a child and, therefore, was simply incapable of demonstrating it to his children.

The truth is I never loved him. I never loved him because he never loved me and instead, demonstrated tyranny and oppression. We were simply in the same home and in each other's way. My purpose was to keep my mouth shut and wash dishes. My sisters were responsible for chores, too, but there was a fixation directed towards me by my father. Unlike my siblings, I was unwilling to bow down in complete, willful, servitude. I did my chores, but I did not worship my father the way that he wanted me to. He would always find fault in something I did or didn't do to his standard and he would compare me negatively to my sisters. Even when the beatings came, my sisters would scream in agony, but I refused. Even as a child, I realized my father's darkness needed our agony as a feeling of control and power. He was a powerless man who derived a sense of power and pleasure in subjecting his daughters to his ritualistic abuse. The darkness and brokenness in his heart fed upon our pain. I learned this early on and, even though he continued to heap more abuse upon me than my sisters, I refused to cry. I knew our verbal screams of pain were what he was beating us for, and I refused, despite the inequity in how he forced his hand more heavily upon me. My sisters would cry and scream and beg for mercy. I did not. I learned to grit through the beatings. He even mentioned it years later, as though it were something humorous, how I refused to cry. There were times I absolutely hated him. I know that. We had calm times. We laughed. Beach vacations were always the best because my father would always be on his best behavior and I could rely on the fact that he typically would leave us alone.

I forgave my father for his abuse and neglect. While it took much more personal trauma work in therapy, I have forgiven my mother for her apathy, delusions, and her willful neglect in refusing to leave my father.

One of my own personal triumphs through my clinical work is gaining the logical understanding of why abuse happens. Now that I have this logical understanding, I can assess my trauma in a different light. I am now more equipped with healthy tools to better identify my own triggers and behaviors related to my trauma. For that alone, I am grateful.

After my father died, one of the outcomes was the realization that while I never loved him, I didn't hate him anymore and I am content with that. I am at peace.

For so many years the anger and hatred and the feelings of inadequacy that I carried around with me and in my heart, were like a physical weight I was unwilling to put down. It affected every aspect of my life. It prevented me from having the ability to be vulnerable and intimate relationships. I didn't know any better and would not know any better for many years to come, until I met a wonderful therapist who helped me to articulate my feelings in a way that unburdened my emotional connection.

Forgiveness is not for the person who has harmed you.

Forgiveness is for you.

Forgiving yourself is even harder. But, it can be achieved once you have done the work and taken ownership of your actions. It is a willful acceptance of accountability in tandem with a promise to yourself to let it go.

No one is perfect. Sometimes people get caught up in behaviors that are cyclical in their toxicity. Sometimes people feel like they must delude themselves in order to just live. It can be seemingly impossible to make necessary changes. I am living proof that it is possible.

It is possible to break the chains of emotional servitude. When someone has hurt you and you carry around your anger towards them, then they still have influence over you. You have the right to absolve yourself of these relationships. You have the right to not tolerate toxicity. You also have the obligation, and with the appropriate amount of time and healing, to forgive and let go and move forward in your life. The only way you can achieve joy and purpose is to forgive.

Forgiveness is derivative of love. It is the channel you want to be watching.

CHAPTER SIXTEEN

GRATITUDE

I am grateful for so many wonderful people, things and experiences in my life.

I am grateful for the adversity and experiences I have had that have taught me how to pay attention to all the many gifts I have received in my life. As I type this, I am sitting here mentally bombarded with so many different experiences that I want to share as an example of gratitude, and I know that I cannot fit them all into these pages. However, one stands out now. 98 steps, if I remember correctly. From the front of my tent to the bathroom tent. It took 98 steps or roughly five minutes to get from my tent in the desert of Prince Sultan Air Base in Saudi Arabia to the female latrine tent. Let me tell you, in the desert where temperatures during the day could hit 130 degrees Fahrenheit regularly, you had to keep yourself hydrated. At night before bed I would often drink a minimum of three bottles of water just to maintain my hydration in the climate-controlled environment of our tent. Mornings were rough to say the least. Waking up with a full bladder and having to throw on appropriate attire for the walk to the toilet was excruciating at times. Since the latrine tent was located next to the shower tent, my morning episode was often accompanied with the internal struggle of "do I grab my shower kit now or just come back later?" Sometimes my bladder would answer the question for me. Twenty-two years later, I still appreciate being able to leave my slumber, hair askew, no bra, and walk ten feet to my toilet to relieve myself and return to the cool sheets of my bed for a few more minutes. I appreciate not being exposed to three-digit temperatures first thing in the morning, but simply being able to wake up in a leisurely manner and find my way to my coffee. I am so grateful for running water, electricity, my own coffee maker with my favorite brand of coffee. I am grateful for having the experience of living in a tent with six other women all those years ago.

Gratitude, much like the expression of love we talked about previously, is also a practice. It's a choice. We can all choose to be grateful. Granted, when we are under stress or are feeling as though our best laid plans will never come to fruition, we can always choose to find gratitude. We just have to know where to look.

Maybe you planned to be more financially independent at this point in your life or, perhaps, the relationship you desired with a particular partner didn't work out. It can feel insurmountable to pull yourself out of a feeling of despair. Remember, each day is a brand-new day. If you decided to finally start losing weight but you slipped up and ate that piece of cheesecake (personal experience), know that you have a responsibility to be kind to yourself and start anew. Be grateful for the cheesecake! Did you enjoy it? (I did.) Moving forward in your journey, no matter what it may be, remember there will be obstacles and roadblocks. Just like a road trip, you just need to re-configure your travel plans. That's all you must do. Be grateful for these obstacles. I know it's difficult, but when you achieve your goals, the obstacles that you have overcome make your success so much sweeter.

It's all about perspective. When we have a healthy perspective, we can cultivate gratitude.

Having gratitude prevents unnecessary stress and can even mitigate depressive episodes.

Have you ever met someone who reminded you of Eeyore from Winnie the Pooh? Isn't it draining to be around someone who is an emotional vacuum? I'm not talking about someone who is dealing with a significant life issue such as grieving the loss of a loved one or divorce or some other heavy issue. I'm talking about the individual who is incessantly negative. We talked previously about toxic people and behaviors. Make no mistake, the "Debbie/Danny downer" is another aspect of this condition. While you may feel compelled to be compassionate towards these individuals who are compulsively negative, remember that it is a behavior that has been cultivated as a measure to manipulate others as a means to gain some sense of connection, albeit in a negative, passive aggressive way. While it is perfectly acceptable, and encouraged at times, to be supportive towards these types of people, it's far more important to be mindful of their unwillingness to let go of their "victim-ness", as it is the currency that they use to create their connection to others. You can always choose to model gratitude for these people without being pulled into their chasm of victimhood. You can do this without expressing any kind of judgment for their state of mind as well.

Maybe you are the "Debbie/Danny downer" in this scenario. If so, do you want to change? Do you want to feel gratitude? In the "Worthiness" chapter, I talk about all the years I spent negating joy in my own life as a measure of not calling attention to myself out of habit. Can you look inward and identify why you maybe at times feel isolated in your despair or despondent attitude? It's ok if you can't. Many of these ideas in this book take a while to germinate. Like a seed needs to absorb water and nutrients from the soil and sunlight, these ideas are like seeds. It's ok if change doesn't happen overnight.

The problem with gratitude

Believe it or not, many people can have issues with gratitude. If a person goes out of their way to help someone, the recipient of that assistance may feel an obligation. It's perfectly acceptable to offer someone a few dollars for helping with a flat tire, or maybe a neighbor notices you left your garage door open. Perhaps a bottle of wine or a gift card to express gratitude for the assistance. Beyond that, there is no obligation. None. Now if someone is in your life who is consistently helping you out in one way or another, then there may be a feeling of obligation.

Are you obligated to anyone?

Do you have a neighbor who always returns your dog when he jumps the fence?

Maybe you have a co-worker who always offers to take your wastebin?

Expression of gratitude must match the overture. If you have a coworker who is consistent in helping, what is something that you can do to return the favor? Does your coworker expect anything in return that you're not interested in giving?

Understanding the motivations behind a person's efforts is key to a proper expression of gratitude. Maybe your coworker wants to ingratiate himself to you as a means of asking you out on a date? It all depends on whether you're interested in your coworker that way. Maybe you have a strict rule about dating at work. Do you continue to allow your coworker to take your wastebin?

Being mindful of the intentions of others is key. It's important to be aware while not being overly suspicious. One or two considerate overtures is appropriate to return with a verbal expression of gratitude. Beyond that, is something that requires further exploration.

Acceptance of favors and assistance

Gratitude is often overlooked if someone is interested in a different outcome. Why do people do what they do for others? Some folks are altruistic by nature and harmless. Others may be creating a climate where they can have an influence in your life. It's always important to be aware of the difference.

Gratitude amid adversity

Imagine being in the middle of a life altering event, such as divorce, loss of a job, death of a loved one, grim medical diagnosis, financial devastation and being able to express a measure of gratitude. It's not easy for sure, but it is possible. It is always a choice. The disappointment, shame, fear, and isolation of these events can cloak the heart of the most well intended person. However, even during these situations, it's vital to at least maintain an awareness of what isn't going wrong at a given moment of crisis. When we trip and fall, we may stay down for a minute, nursing our wounds and feeling as though it's not worth getting up because "you're just going to fall down again". However, the key to survival in any of this is to realize that while wounded, you can still have gratitude. You can be pissed off that your partner left you for someone else and still be grateful you can afford to live in your house alone or your children are safe and healthy. You can be disappointed you lost your job but grateful you have plenty of savings in the bank or that you can sell your house and move into that smaller apartment near the waterfront. Sometimes discovering your cancer has metastasized is the motivation you need to take that trip to Africa while you still can.

You can feel two emotions at once. It's not about denying your disappointment or anger and opting for gratitude as your elected emotion. That's delusional and we don't want that. All I am saying is maintain levity in your emotional position. Hold space for your anger or your fear, but be aware that the sky isn't in fact falling on your head. Hold space for your disappointment that your marriage ended but know that you'll move onward and will find a new path while expressing gratitude for the opportunity to make decisions in your life without having to ask someone else what their opinion is. Even a grim diagnosis can motivate a person to look inward and evolve towards their goals in life, albeit more expeditiously, than they had ever intended.

I don't know if I would appreciate the time with my grandparents on their small rural Alabama acreage as a child had I not been so burdened with the hardship of dealing with an abusive homelife. To this day, scuppernong grapes are a thing of the past. I've never been able to find any anywhere, as my grandmother had a vine planted behind the house. It's just as well, I suppose, as I cannot imagine finding any that would replicate the experience of being able to pick them in the mid-day Alabama summer heat, biting into one and having the hot sour-sweetness become the tasty reminder that I was safe. I don't even know if they are available at farmers markets. I've never seen them, but I can't imagine they would even come close to my grandmother's. My gratitude and appreciation for this aspect of my childhood runs deep because of my ability to compare it to my adversity. Early morning visits to the hen house, the grass dewy under our feet, and the humid air carrying notes of pecan and manure all encapsulate my sense of childhood safety. I am grateful to have had beautiful, devout and faithful grandparents who colored my world with these gentle reminders that my life was meaningful and worthwhile. I don't know what choices I would have made in my life were it not for their balance against the torrential experience of my childhood. I am grateful.

My healthy, happy, intelligent, thoughtful, and caring children make me grateful every day. No matter what else I accomplish in my life, I know that my greatest achievements are already here. They do good things and make the world a better place. They, and they alone, are my one true purpose. I am so deeply grateful for them. I am grateful they are happy and healthy people. I am grateful that they see the world through grateful and kind eyes.

Despite the dissolution of our marriage, I am grateful for my ex-husband. Our relationship has been a rocky one and, while it evolved into something different, I am deeply grateful for having it. He has always challenged me, both through intentional and most often unintentional ways of doing better. He always believed in me, and whether he expressed it explicitly, his actions were always an indication that he knew who and what I was well before I did. I am grateful for this. I am grateful for him and I am grateful for what our relationship has now become.

I am grateful for our son's birth father for obvious reasons. We were never meant to be and that's ok. I got the best part of the deal and for the first six years of his life, I didn't have to share him with anyone. I am grateful for that experience. Having been a single mother was my glimpse into learning how to self-love. It started with my unconditional love for my baby (detailed at length in the Love chapter) but then evolved into my willingness to love myself for my baby and then for myself. Without this experience I have no doubt that I would not be where I am today. I am grateful for this experience.

What are you grateful for? How have your experiences shaped your view of the world and yourself? Are there aspects of your life that you'd like to be more grateful for?

CHAPTER SEVENTEEN

CONCLUSION

My hope for you is that you have been able to find answers to questions you've held in your heart over the years. While there is no book available to permanently cure the long-term effects of trauma, my continued hope is that you have begun a journey of healing that won't just stop with this book.

I pride myself on being a good therapist and I would even assert that most clinicians go into this work with the same intentions. However, I encourage you to continue to seek out answers. Whether that is by finding other books to read or by cultivating a rapport with a professional counselor. Remember, you get to decide what is helpful and what isn't. Keep reading but always seek the treatment of a professional along the way. Experiencing trauma is but one aspect of mental unwellness. There are genetic predispositions that can adversely affect your sense of wellbeing too.

Always seek the advice of a licensed therapist during your journey.

Never stop learning. Never stop growing and healing. Remember to be kind to yourself and allow space for mistakes.

Do the work. Take the time. Make the changes you need to make. Clean up your messes.

Experience healing. Cultivate joy. Flip the channel and live your life on your terms.

I wish you peace and fulfillment in all your endeavors!

Love, Alma